THE DARWEN COUNTY HISTORY SERIES

A History of Norfolk

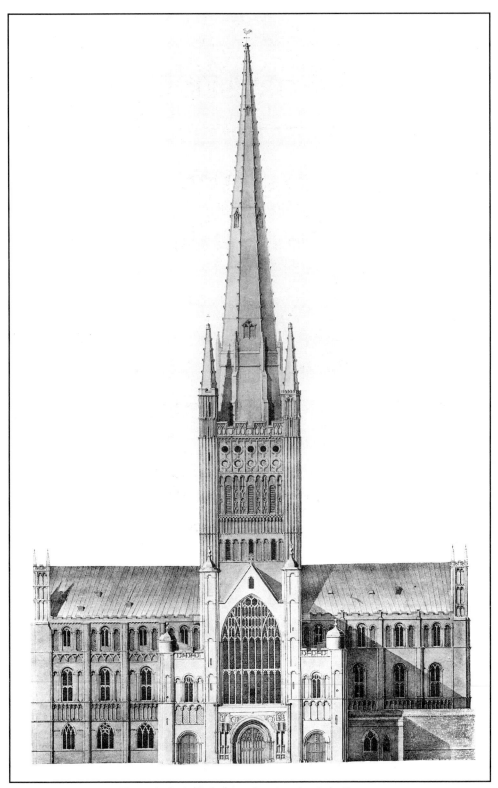

Norwich Cathedral, west elevation, by J.A. Repton.

**THE DARWEN COUNTY
HISTORY SERIES**

A History of
Norfolk

Susanna Wade Martins

drawings by Sue White

Phillimore

1997

Published by
PHILLIMORE & CO. LTD.
Shopwyke Manor Barn, Chichester, West Sussex

First published 1984
Second edition 1997

ISBN 1 86077 014 2

Printed and bound in Great Britain by
BUTLER AND TANNER LTD.
Frome, Somerset

Contents

List of Illustrations

Frontispiece :   Norwich Cathedral

List of Colour Illustrations

Acknowledgements

This book could not have been written without the help of a great many people and organisations. Andrew Lawson, Tony Gregory, Robert Rickett and Kenneth Penn of the Norfolk Archaeological Unit all read and gave helpful advice on the early chapters, while Derek Edwards, also of the Norfolk Archaeological Unit, helped with the selection of the aerial photographs. Elizabeth and Paul Rutledge helped with the chapter on Medieval towns and Susan and David Yaxley with the Tudor and Stuart period. Mary Manning read and advised on the chapters about more recent industrial history, while Dr. Roger Virgoe and Dr. Richard Wilson helped with chapters on the medieval church and agricultural history. John Ayton brought his expertise from the County Planning Department to the reading of the last chapter. However, all the opinions expressed in this book are my own and I must take full responsibility for any errors that remain. Finally, the whole project would have been abandoned long before completion without the constant help and encouragement of my husband, Peter.

I would like to thank the following for permission to reproduce illustrations: The Society of Antiquaries, frontispiece; Norfolk Air Photography Library of Norfolk Museums Service and Derek A. Edwards I, II, III, IV, V, VI, VII, VIII, XI, XII, 18, 39, 82, 88, 97, 101; Norfolk Museums Service, Field Archaeology Division, 20, 21, 22, 23, 37; Field Archaeology Division/Norfolk Archaeological Trust, 15; Norfolk Museums Service, Norwich Castle Museum, 56, 58, 75, 77, 125; the late Hallam Ashley, 83; Barbara Cornford, 87; Cambridge University air photography collection, 57; John Mitchell, University of East Anglia, 70; Strutt and Parker, 96; Norfolk Museums Service, Strangers' Hall, 155, 157; Nicholas Hill, 79; Lord Cholmodeley, 76; Norfolk Museums Service, Rural Life Museum, Gressenhall, 84, 85, 89, 100, 132, 162; Chris Mullen, 90; Norfolk Museums Service, Great Yarmouth Museums, 120; Alan Sewell, 170; Eastern Counties Newpapers, 123, 146; Colman's of Norwich, 130, 131, 147; Tate Gallery, 114; Local Studies Library, Norwich, 115, 156, 159; Jarrolds, 139; School of Fine Arts, University of East Anglia, 171.

North Elmham
August 1995   SUSANNA WADE MARTINS, Ph.D.

Every land and every sea
Have I crossed but much the worst
Is the land of Norfolk cursed ...
Satan on the way to Hell
Ruined Norfolk as he fell.

Translated by Professor Peter Ashley from *Anonymi Petroburgenis descriptio Norfolciensium* (12th century)

Let any stranger find me out so pleasant a county, such good ways, large heaths, three such places as Norwich, Yarmouth and Lynn in any county of England and I'll be once again a vagabond and visit them.

Sir Thomas Browne (17th century)

1

Prehistoric Norfolk

Much that sets Norfolk apart from the rest of the British Isles is the result of geographical factors and its isolation from the rest of Britain, while access from Scandinavia and northern Europe was very much easier. This continental link was never stronger than at the beginning of man's history when much of the North Sea and the fens were dry land, and Britain was part of Europe. Then the area which is now East Anglia was often penetrated by people moving west from Northern Europe, and north across what is now the Channel, from France.

The early history of man in the British Isles is dominated by the climate. Between 500,000 and 8,000 years B.C. Britain experienced ice ages, each lasting thousands of years, and in two of these, the Anglian and the Wolstonian, Norfolk was entirely covered by ice. Our earliest evidence for man in Norfolk is for the period between these two—about 400,000 B.C. We know of his existence, not from his shelters, but from his tools, made from locally-found flints. Both the flint core and the flakes chipped off were used. Core tools include axes, scrapers and cutters, and knives were made from the flakes. Over 200 find spots for these tools are known in Norfolk. Although this may appear to be a large number, they are all that has been found so far to demonstrate man's presence over a period of about 125,000 years. From pollen analysis we know that at this time Norfolk was an area of mixed birch and pine woodland, where hunting and plant gathering were the most important activities. Bones of straight-tusked elephants, deer, rhinoceroses, pigs, horses and beavers have all been found.

With the arrival of the Wolstonian ice sheet, about 225,000 years ago, the hunters moved south, and for 100,000 years, Norfolk was again a frozen tundra. As the ice sheet melted and retreated north it left behind it boulder clay, loams, sands and gravels which now cover much of the county. The heavy boulder clays are mainly in the centre and south and have always formed a distinctive region. Before clearance, in the Iron Age and later, they would have supported thick woodland and, once cleared, formed an area difficult to drain and to farm profitably. To the north-east of this area the peri-glacial soils are lighter. The woods were not so dense as those on the boulder clays, so were easier for early farmers to clear. Even lighter soils were deposited in the west. The sandy breckland soils have never been much good for agriculture, and until recent afforestation, presented a wild heathland landscape. To the north,

1 *Early Palaeolithic hand-axe from Carrow.*

2 *Neolithic pottery and stone implements from Norfolk sites.*

Mesolithic fish-spear found at sea 25 miles N.E. of Cromer; Microlith point from Kelling Heath; Reconstruction of Mesolithic arrow

3   Mesolithic weapons.

the soils are still poor, but with careful farming have become good cereal lands. Running north to south across the west of the county is a chalk ridge covered by a very thin layer of glacial deposits. This has always been an area of relatively open country, and early on became a routeway linking Norfolk to the south of England. All these sub-regions have played an important part in the development of the county throughout its history.

By 8,000 B.C. the climate was beginning to become milder, although still cooler than today. Dwarf birch and willow were replaced by mixed woodland on the light land and alder and oak on the heavier soils. The mammoth and woolly rhinoceros died out, leaving aurochs (wild oxen), giant Irish elks, deer and wild boar for men to hunt.

From about 8,000 B.C. new groups of people were moving from the Continent into eastern England. It was not until 7,000-6,000 B.C. that the rising sea level finally cut the land link between Britain and Europe, and Norfolk covered a much larger area than at any time since. The cliffs along the east coast are constantly being eroded, and so the coast line of the New Stone Age must have been well seaward of the present line.

Settlements dating from between 6,500 and 3,500 B.C. have been found at Kelling Heath, between Holt and Cromer, and at Hellesdon, Sparham and Lyng on the gravel along the Wensum valley. After about 9,000 B.C. communities in the Near East had gradually ceased to rely entirely on hunting and food gathering for their sustenance and began to cultivate crops and domesticate animals. Men also began to make pots of clay—important to archaeologists as they are one of the few Neolithic artifacts to survive. There are many varieties of pot, and distinctive styles indicate contact between different groups. Pottery from about 4,500 B.C. has been found at Sparham, Edingthorpe, Brettenham, Eaton Heath, Broome Heath and Spong Hill. We know that barley and emmer (a primitive form of wheat) were grown, and crab apples and hazel nuts collected for food. From animal bones it is clear that cattle, pigs, sheep and goats were kept.

Pottery is not the only indication of a higher technological level. Flint implements were now polished smooth instead of being left with a rough surface. All over Neolithic Britain, men were building long barrows in which to bury their dead, and a few have been located in Norfolk, at Ditchingham, West Rudham, Harpley and Felthorpe. Some of these remain as only slight humps in the ground, and others have been ploughed away. Even so, there were never enough barrows to allow for the majority of the population to have been buried in them. Perhaps they were reserved for chieftains, which suggests a tribal hierarchy. Only one, at West Rudham, has been excavated. It was constructed of turf and covered with a layer of thick gravel, but did not appear to have any internal divisions; no bones or cremated remains were found. At Arminghall we can see the remains of a wooden henge monument, which from the air appears as a horseshoe of massive posts set within a ditch. Henges are usually late Neolithic in date and this is one of the earliest in Britain, built about 3,250 B.C.

4   Gold ornament from Caister-on-Sea. Late Bronze Age.

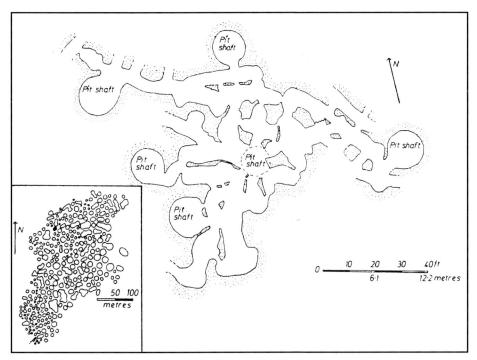

The most important source of flints in Norfolk was Grimes Graves, near Thetford. The flint mines covered about 90 acres and at least 500 shafts have been found, as well as 1,600 shallow pits which were used for opencast mining. The mines were at their busiest just after 2,000 B.C., when the population was rising and increasing the demand for stone axes. Some of the shafts were cut to a depth of 12 metres, with galleries often linked to each other and radiating from the main shaft. There must have been a highly institutionalised and professional mining community here, which supported other industries such as those making baskets and providing the 50,000 antler picks used for excavation which have so far been found.

A new type of pottery appeared in Norfolk about 2,500 B.C.; this was 'beaker pottery', tall beaker-type pots, often ornamented with geometric designs, which are also found in the Rhineland and thus demonstrate the connections between East Anglia and the Low Countries. It is probable that the people who brought beaker pottery also introduced the use of bronze. Copper was the first metal to be smelted by prehistoric man, but the alloy of tin and copper—bronze—produces a stronger product, and by 1,600 B.C. bronze had completely replaced copper. By 1,400 B.C. metal was becoming far more readily available. The palstave, a sort of axe for felling trees, was widely used. The distribution of their find spots suggests that the clay soils of central and southern Norfolk were now being brought into cultivation. The only monuments remaining from the Bronze Age are the round barrows which were built over the graves of the dead; the sites of over 1,000 are now known in Norfolk.

6 *Early Bronze Age grave goods from a barrow at Little Cressingham.*

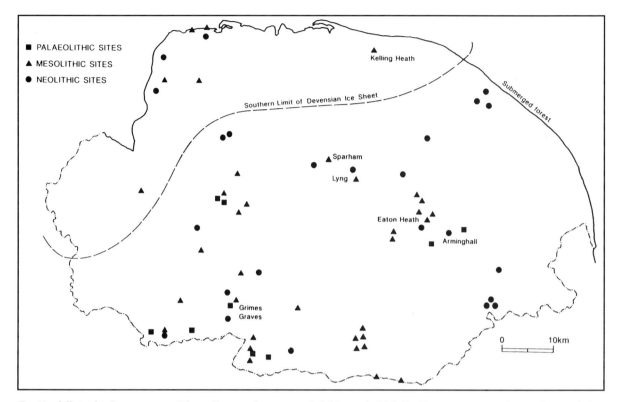

- ■ PALAEOLITHIC SITES
- ▲ MESOLITHIC SITES
- ● NEOLITHIC SITES

Kelling Heath

Southern Limit of Devensian Ice Sheet

Submerged forest

Sparham

Lyng

Eaton Heath

Arminghall

Grimes
Graves

0   10km

7 *Norfolk in the Stone Ages (based on information from* An Historical Atlas of Norfolk *and drawn by Phillip Judge).*

8 *Ring terminal from one of the Snettisham gold torques.*

The climate between 2,000 and 900 B.C. appears to have been drier than previously, and on the fen edge of Norfolk there is a remarkable concentration of occupation sites. Arrowheads suggest that wild-fowling may have been important; leather working tools show that cattle were kept, and cereals were grown. These areas could well have been very wet in the winter, and their occupation may have been seasonal. Gradually the climate became wetter, probably at its wettest between 850 and 650 B.C., when forest clearances were being carried out on a large scale.

About 1,500 B.C. new influences from the Wessex region can be seen to be affecting the lifestyle of the peoples of Norfolk. We know of this from burials, such as that at Little Cressingham, containing bronze daggers, gold ornaments and amber beads in the Wessex fashion. Many of the possessions in these graves must have come to Norfolk by trade. The importance of trade is also shown by another site typical of the period—the hoard, consisting of groups of metal objects buried together by a trader or craftsman. Over 80 Middle and Late Bronze Age hoards have been found in Norfolk. Implements include axes, spearheads, palstaves, sickles, saws, swords, chisels, gouges and shields. There are also ornaments, including bracelets, finger rings, pins and torcs. In the Middle Bronze Age the ornaments tend to be of Danish or Germanic origin, whilst later they come from central Europe and northern France.

Iron had been in use in central Europe for about 300 years before it reached Norfolk, *c.*650 B.C. Unfortunately, most Iron Age implements have rusted away in the ground, and we know more about Iron Age cultures from pottery, of which a great variety has been found. Probably both iron implements and the new types of pottery were introduced by traders. The only complete Iron Age building to be excavated in Norfolk is at West Harling. Bones found show that cattle and sheep were kept, their meat being supplemented by wild pig and deer. Dogs were kept, for work, or perhaps for food. Querns and seed impressions on pottery suggest that wheat was grown, and loom weights show that weaving was carried out. Although we know something of the way of life of these early Iron Age people, we know nothing about their religion, or the rituals associated with burials.

About the middle of the third century B.C., new influences began to reach East Anglia from the Marne region of France. Chariots and superior weaponry were imported: a sword found in a third-century grave at Shouldham shows the fine craftsmanship of the Marnian smiths.

Hill-forts are very rare in eastern England, and only five are known in Norfolk. Except for Warham, which has a double ditch, they are all simple single-ditch enclosures with nothing to compare with sites like Maiden Castle in Dorset. Some may be as early as Late Bronze Age and others might be as late as the Saxon period. The existence of hill-forts implies that there was a need for defence, which suggests competition for the available resources. There must have been some form of social organisation and authority to bring about the erection of hill-forts; units

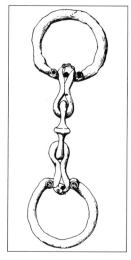

9 *Bronze bridle bit from Ringstead.*

10 *Norfolk in the Bronze and Iron Ages (based on information from* An Historical Atlas of Norfolk *and drawn by Phillip Judge).*

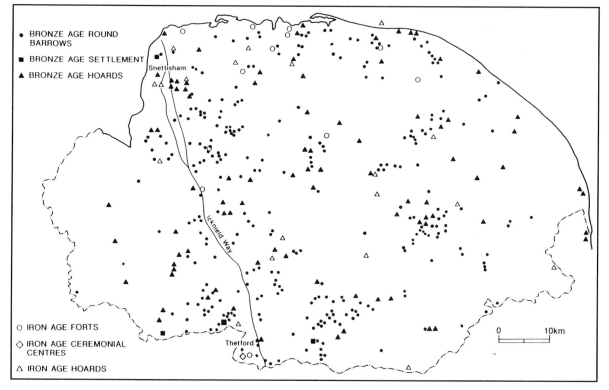

- ● BRONZE AGE ROUND BARROWS
- ■ BRONZE AGE SETTLEMENT
- ▲ BRONZE AGE HOARDS

Snettisham

Icknield Way

○ IRON AGE FORTS
◇ IRON AGE CEREMONIAL CENTRES
△ IRON AGE HOARDS

Thetford

0   10km

11 *Early Bronze Age handled beaker from a burial at Bodney*

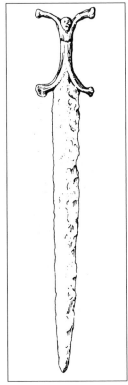

12 *Iron Age sword from a grave at Shouldham.*

of settlement larger than the single farmstead must have developed by the time the forts were built.

By the late first century A.D., coins bearing the names of the royal house of the Iceni were being minted. We do not know who the Iceni were, or when they first established their kingdom. They were certainly wealthy. Lavish ornaments made from precious metals have been found in hoards at Ringstead and Snettisham. More than 50 torcs and bracelets have been found in Norfolk, more than from the rest of Britain put together, as well as other jewellery, weapons and horse accoutrements. Chariots were widely used by the nobility. Finds of Icenian coins are concentrated in the Thetford area, and this may therefore have been the site of their capital. A very late Iron Age group of round houses, standing within a heavily defended rectangular ditched enclosure has recently been excavated at Gallows Hill, and this may have been the major Iceni stronghold.

The tribes of southern Britain were constantly at war with each other in the years leading up to the Roman invasion. Sometime between 20 and 15 B.C., the Catuvellauni of Cambridgeshire and Hertfordshire became dominant over the Trinovantes of Essex and south Suffolk. The Catuvellauni eventually became the most powerful kingdom in Britain, and were ready to march against the Iceni when the Romans landed on the south coast in A.D. 43. The kingdoms south of the Thames were quickly defeated, and the Romans marched north to confront the Catuvellauni, who were also defeated.

The Iceni had probably already formed an alliance with Rome, and managed to remain an independent kingdom. Roman goods began to appear in Norfolk, and Roman coins replaced local ones. However, the peaceful position of the Iceni as a client kingdom ended violently in A.D. 60. It was customary for client kings to leave their lands to the Emperor, but King Prasutagus tried to leave Nero only half, dividing the rest between his two daughters. The Roman army took advantage of the situation to overrun the area. The King's widow, Boudicca, led a revolt which was rapidly supported by the Trinovantes. The rebels captured the Romanised town of Camulodunum (Colchester) and laid it waste, and also destroyed Verulamium (St Albans) and Londinium (London). The majority of the Roman forces had been in Anglesey when the revolt broke out; they met the rebels somewhere north-west of London and quickly defeated them. Boudicca died, probably by her own hand, and the kingdom of the Iceni was at an end. The Romans took revenge in Norfolk by sacking, burning and looting. After this Norfolk was part of the great Roman Empire which stretched from the Middle East to Scotland.

13 *A Norfolk barrow, from a 19th-century painting.*

2

Roman and Anglo-Saxon Norfolk

It was not until after the Boudiccan rebellion that Romanisation really began in Norfolk. There followed 200 peaceful years which encouraged economic and social development, when southern Britain for the first and last time was part of an empire covering most of western Europe, with a common language and culture.

14 *Roman soldier.*

By the end of the first century A.D. all the major Roman roads in Norfolk had been built, one of the earliest (*c*.A.D. 70) being from Colchester to the new capital of the Iceni at Caistor St Edmunds, well away from the probable site of the traditional tribal centre at Thetford. One of the most important through-routes was the Peddar's Way (A.D. 70-100), which linked north Essex with the Wash and Lincoln-shire. The major roads through the area were built first, forming the infrastructure for the centralised administration of a military state, while smaller ones, sometimes following ancient routes like the Icknield Way, were developed later to serve economic needs.

The earliest planned Roman town was *Venta Icenorum* at Caistor St Edmunds, which probably controlled an area covering north-west Suffolk as well as the whole of present-day Norfolk. The old tribal aristocracy were in charge of local affairs, levying local taxation and also imperial taxes to be sent to Rome. The town was laid out about A.D. 70, at first consisting of no more than a few timber structures. However, by A.D. 125 it was prosperous enough to allow the erection of a stone forum and basilica, and a bath house. Later in the century two temples were built side by side, and a third was built outside the walls about A.D. 200. As the town's administrative importance grew so did its industries. Four early pottery kilns have been found and there is evidence for glass-making, spinning and weaving. The population may have risen to about a thousand, and new houses, although still of wattle and daub, were erected on masonry footings. There is some evidence that the town had both a water supply and a sewerage system. Permanent fortifications were not built until the third century, when 35 acres were enclosed; on the north side the walls were 11 feet thick and they still stand to a height of 19 feet.

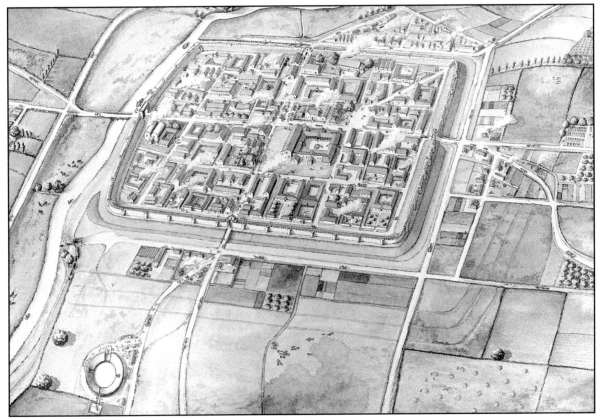

15 Venta Icenorum *(Caister-by-Norwich), reconstruction drawing by Sue White.*

About the time that *Venta Icenorum* was acquiring its first public buildings, a new port was founded near the mouth of the Yare at Caister-on-Sea. Its position marks the shortest sea crossing from the Rhine, and its creation shows that by the early second century Norfolk was a growing market for imported goods.

Other settlements and market towns grew up, particularly at crossroads, one good example being that of Brampton, where a pottery was at its height in the second century. Brampton ware found its way to the north of England. Other crossroad sites have been identified at Saham Toney, Billingford, Kempstone, Toftrees and possibly Denver. A roadside settlement grew up at Scole on the Colchester-Caistor St Edmunds road, originally as a military staging post.

16 *Reconstruction of a temple of the type found at* Venta Icenorum.

The majority of people in Roman Norfolk were small farmers living either in villages or isolated farmsteads, such as that at Runcton Holme. Most of their pottery was home-made, and the peasants were little influenced by Roman culture until the second century, when some Roman pottery appeared. This was probably typical of many villages.

The fenland was a densely populated area; a drier phase in the area's history seems to have begun about the middle of the first century, and settlement became large-scale between A.D. 100 and 150. This was imperial property, as it was virgin territory, and was either let out to tenants or managed direct by a crown agent. Salt production, an important local industry, was an imperial monopoly. Fields here tended to be rather small and clustered round the settlement, probably gardens or stock-yards rather than arable land. By the third century, however, flooding had become a problem at Welney and Hockwold, and the population declined. With the breakdown of Roman authority in the early fifth century, the drains were not maintained and the fenland was abandoned. Early Anglo-Saxon settlers were not attracted by an overgrown land-scape of choked drains and crumbling dwellings, and the area was not resettled until the eighth or ninth centuries. The settlements within the fens contrast with those along the edge, where the villas of a rich and privileged minority were sited. In the Methwold, Feltwell, and Hockwold districts, there were several villas with bathrooms, and two temple sites at Hockwold.

Across the chalklands of west Norfolk there was a far denser population in the Roman period than before, but in villas rather than towns or large villages. The sites at Grimston and Gayton Thorpe remain to show that they were well appointed with mosaic floors, painted walls

17 *Roman Norfolk (based on information from* An Historical Atlas of Norfolk *and drawn by Phillip Judge).*

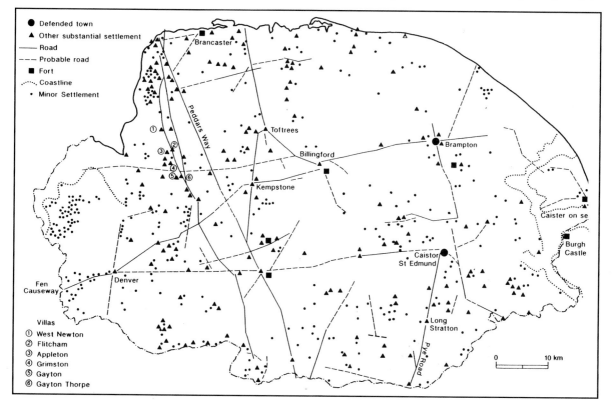

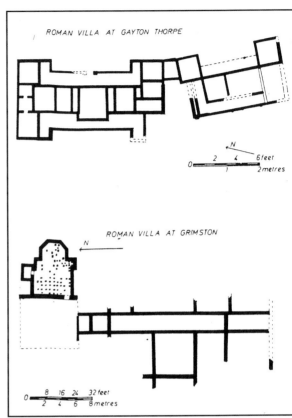

18 Above. *Aerial view of the Saxon shore fort at Brancaster*, above left. *The rectangular fort with the crop marks of some buildings is in the foreground and the crop marks of the extra-mural settlement can be seen behind.*

19 Above right. *Roman villas at Gayton Thorpe and Grimston*, above right.

and underfloor heating. These were probably the centres of large working farms in the third and fourth centuries. There were several industrial sites in west Norfolk, including an ironworking centre at Ashwicken in the second century; however, it can only ever have produced small quantities, as the method used was very wasteful. Pottery kilns were working at Pentney in the third century and at Shouldham in the third and fourth. Loom weights found at Denver show that weaving took place there.

The peaceful conditions which encouraged economic development were interrupted from the third century onwards, and it became necessary to build forts against raids from the sea. Brancaster, one of the earliest, was first laid out at the end of the second century, probably under military authority. The later fort on the site was built about 225. It formed part of a line of defences constructed from the Wash to the Solent during the third century to defend the eastern and southern coasts of Britain against Saxon raiders. The fort at Burgh Castle and the fortified town of Caister-on-Sea guarded the Yare estuary and the river route to the local capital. Burgh Castle is about the same size as Brancaster. Its massive walls have survived on three sides. Today it stands four miles inland, but in the Roman period there was a harbour outside the western wall.

Shielded by the Roman fleet and the coastal fortresses, East Anglia remained prosperous until the first half of the fourth century, but from then on economic decline is apparent. The civilian settlement at Brancaster was almost deserted; the villas of Gayton Thorpe and Appleton were abandoned, and *Venta Icenorum's* prosperity declined. Many fenland farms were given up. The sequence of events in the late fourth and early fifth centuries is far from clear, but by 420 the Roman army no longer occupied Britain.

We do not know whether there was any Saxon settlement in East Anglia whilst it was still part of the Roman Empire; no firm evidence for the employment of Saxon mercenaries by the Romans has been found here. The mid-fifth century, however, marks the beginning of a period of substantial immigration. Little is known of the new-comers' way of life, and very few of their houses have been found in Norfolk. The distribution of Anglo-Saxon cemeteries indicates their settlement patterns. They are found along the river valleys and near the coast and fen edge, but not in the central claylands. We know little of what happened to the native population; there were great changes at the top of Roman society, but perhaps far less at the bottom.

The earliest Saxon arrivals cremated their dead; about 700 urns were found at Caistor St Edmunds, and over 2,000 have come from Spong Hill near North Elmham. Sometimes small personal possessions like jewellery were not burnt but put into the urns with the ashes. Much more survives when the body is buried rather than burnt; weapons and jewellery remain even when bones dissolve in acid soil. Two of a small group of burials excavated at Swaffham have neatly cut holes in the skull, indicating trepanning as a brain surgery technique, perhaps to let out evil spirits. Other examples have been found at Watton and Grimston.

As the new immigrants took over large areas, they had to defend themselves against each other. It is likely that the five dykes and

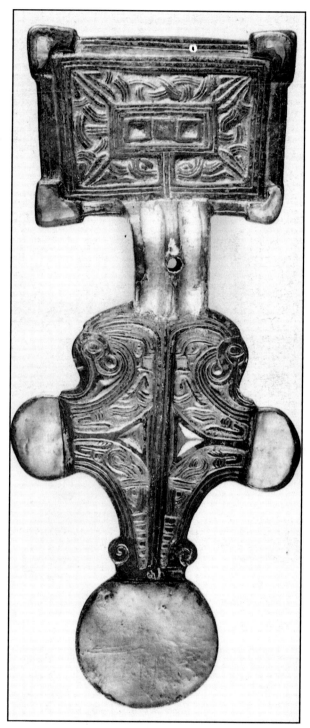

20 *Sixth-century square-headed brooch from Morningthorpe pagan Saxon cemetery.*

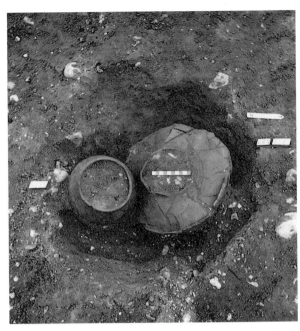

21 Left. *Seated figure on the lid of a cremation urn, from Spong Hill pagan Saxon cemetery.*

22 Above. *Cremation urns being excavated at Spong Hill pagan Saxon cemetery.*

23 Below. *Middle Saxon house with late Saxon burials during excavations at North Elmham.*

banks built in Norfolk date from this period (the late fifth and early sixth centuries). They all cross and defend Roman roads, which shows that these were still important communication links. The two eastern ditches face the two western ones, showing that they represent the defences of two opposing regions.

The contemporary historian, Bede, states that a royal seat was located near Rendlesham in Suffolk. Traditionally, Wehha, who was probably one of the leaders of his people when they migrated to Britain, controlled the immediate region by the mid-sixth century. His son, Wuffa, gave his name to the dynasty and extended its power over the whole East Anglian region. The most powerful East Anglian ruler was Raedwald, who was overlord or 'Bretwalda' of all southern Britain from 610-24, and who may be commemorated by the magnificent ship burial at Sutton Hoo, which shows the wealth of the dynasty in the years immediately before its conversion to Christianity.

24 *South-east tower Burgh Castle, from a drawing of 1859.*

In 597 St Augustine arrived in Kent from Rome, and converted King Aethelbert to Christianity. Sometime later (about 616) Raedwald was baptised whilst visiting Aethelbert, but this may have been little more than a political expedient, as we know that he simply put up a Christian altar next to his pagan ones. More important for the spread of the new religion in East Anglia was the baptism of his son Sigbert, who encouraged Christianity after his accession. At his request, St Felix was sent to East Anglia, and Sigbert gave him a site for his mission at *Dommoc*, which may have been at Dunwich or at the Roman fort of Walton Castle near Felixstowe. Both sites have now been washed away. Felix remained Bishop of East Anglia for 17 years, and spread the gospel to north and south, probably travelling by sea. The first church founded in Norfolk may have been the church at Babingley, dedicated to St Felix, although the present structure is medieval.

We know that by about 680 Christianity was so well established that it was decided to split the East Anglian see in two, and by 803 the northern see was sited at 'Elmham', almost certainly North Elmham and the site may have been chosen because it was near one of the river crossings of the main east-to-west Roman road. Also, the size of the pagan Saxon cemetery there suggests that it may already have been an important religious centre.

Felix and his priests were not the only missionaries working in seventh-century East Anglia. About 631, King Sigbert welcomed the Irish monk Fursey and gave him a site for a monastery at Burgh Castle. From here, Fursey was said to have 'converted many people by his preaching'. We do not know how long his monastery remained, but it was sacked by Mercian raiders about 650, and there was no further Celtic influence on the East Anglian church.

After Sigbert's death the throne passed to a nephew of Raedwald's, Anna, a devout Christian. His daughters founded several abbeys; they themselves had gone to nunneries abroad, which suggests that there were none in Norfolk. The princess Etheldreda founded a monastery for

25 *Glass vessels, found at Burgh Castle.*

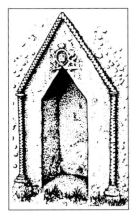

26 *Saxon west door-way, Great Dunham church.*

27 *Pagan Saxon Norfolk (based on information from* An Historical Atlas of Norfolk, *and drawn by Phillip Judge).*

both men and women at Ely in 637, and Anna's youngest daughter Withberga founded a small nunnery at Dereham—whether East or West Dereham is uncertain. There are many legends about her, including one that at a time of severe food shortage two wild does attached themselves to the nunnery to provide milk, a story which explains the saint's emblem of a deer.

We know very little about the church in East Anglia during the eighth century. No documents survive, probably because the monasteries were destroyed and the sees disbanded after the Viking raids of the ninth century. One local bishop visited Rome, and others attended church synods. A manuscript was copied for King Alfred in East Anglia. These scraps of information suggest that books and scholars were to be found there.

If we are short of information on ecclesiastical affairs, there is even less on other matters. The only houses excavated are at North Elmham. They were all rectangular with foundation trenches holding wallposts spaced fairly close together. The spaces between the posts were filled with wattle and daub. There was a central hearth, and often a small room opened off the main one. These houses are a great improvement on the simple dwellings of the pagan Saxon period.

Where archaeological fieldwork has been carried out, settlements with pottery dating from about 650 to 850 have been found in about two-thirds of the present-day parishes, which suggests that the eighth

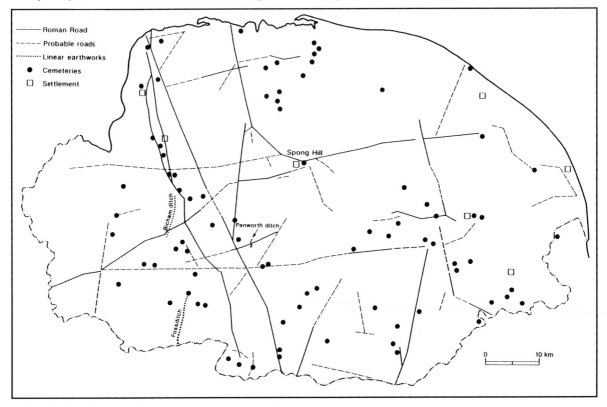

century was a time of steady growth, with new settlements and the area of cultivation increasing. However, these sites rarely coincide with those of modern villages, which have often moved within their parishes.

Another type of evidence for the spread of settlements is that of place-names. Those ending in -*ham* and -*ing* and -*ingham* usually suggest an early settlement; often the -*ham* villages became medieval market towns. In the Launditch area villages with -*tun* endings seem to be later, and, unlike the -*ham* group, two-thirds of these are now deserted; this suggests that they were founded during a phase of expansion into marginal land.

We do not know much about the development of the two major towns of Saxon Norfolk—Thetford and Norwich—in the eighth century. Norwich probably consisted of linear growth along the Wensum, later developing into several small settlements. The name *Northwic* first appears on coins of Aethelstan I (920-40),

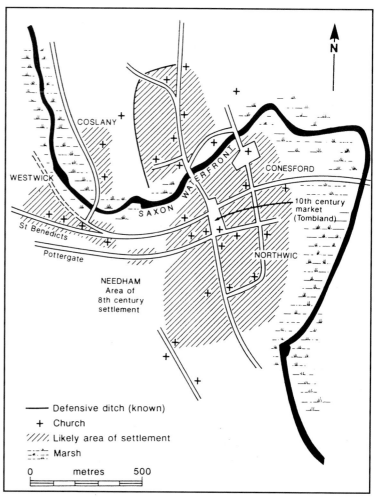

28 *Saxon Norwich.*

although it is thought to be older. It probably referred to a settlement found under the present Cathedral Close. The names *Westwic* and *Coslania*, which survive in street names, also date from this period. The first documentary evidence for the existence of Thetford is in 870, but there was certainly some occupation by the eighth century, again probably little more than a few farmsteads.

During this phase of expansion up to the ninth century, there were constant raids, firstly from Mercia to the west and then, increasingly, from Denmark and Norway. The superb seamanship and fighting qualities of the Scandinavian peoples made them formidable enemies and East Anglia was now the smallest and weakest English kingdom. By the middle of the century there were large-scale Viking landings. In 869 the raiders did not leave for the winter but occupied Thetford, which suggests that it had become a substantial town. It provided a natural base for raids into Mercia, and then into Wessex, which continued until the Vikings were beaten by Alfred at the battle of Edington in 879.

29 *Silver mount from pagan Saxon grave, Morningthorpe.*

The Danish raids resulted in the destruction of monasteries and the end of the East Anglian sees: there is a gap in the list of Elmham bishops of nearly 100 years, until 955. The last king of East Anglia, Edmund, was captured, tortured and finally beheaded, probably at Hellesdon near Norwich although Bury St Edmunds in Suffolk is also a possible location. From 870 to 920 East Anglia was under Danish control, and in 886 the situation was regularised by Alfred's treaty with the Danish leader Guthrum, by which England was divided between them. Eastern England north of the Thames became the 'Danelaw'. The term originally meant that in that area Danish rather than English laws applied. It is very difficult to know how much effect Danish rule had on daily life. In 886 Guthrum had become a Christian, and so had gone some way towards accepting Anglo-Saxon traditions.

It is impossible to be certain how many new settlements were established, but it is known that the Danish fighting men were joined by other settlers from their homeland. Place-names ending in *-by* or *-thorp* are Danish in origin, although *-thorp* usually indicates a secondary settlement. There are 21 *-by* names listed in the Norfolk Domesday, many concentrated in the Flegg district to the east. Very often they are not on the best land, but on that not yet exploited by the Saxons. *-toft* and *-thwaite* are also Danish endings. The Danes were known as 'aescmann' or 'flottmann' to the Saxons, names preserved in Ashmanhaugh and Newton Flotmann. Street names of Scandinavian origin are quite common: *-gate* is the Danish word for street and is preserved in Norwich's Pottergate, to cite only one of many examples.

In recent years the number of Viking finds from Norfolk has increased with about 200 pieces of metal work known, including jewellery and household goods. Most striking are the gold alloy Thor's hammer from South Lopham and decorative plaque showing a mounted warrior, from Bylaugh. One possible lasting influence was that in many Danelaw counties Domesday lists a class of persons only rarely found elsewhere—sokemen and freemen, who made up 41 per cent of the Norfolk population in 1086.

By 917 most of Norfolk was once again under English control with the Danish defeat by Edward the Elder. For the post-Viking period there is much more information available, and archaeological evidence suggests that the period up to the Norman Conquest was one of expansion and increasing prosperity. Small farms grew into villages and some entirely new settlements appeared.

Thetford was at its most important at this time. It had its own mint by the reign of Edgar (959-75), and was a centre of industrial activity from the mid-ninth century, with bronze, iron and pottery which was traded over much of eastern England. By the late 10th century Thetford ranked with Cambridge, Norwich and Ipswich as a town 'of such liberty and dignity that if anyone bought land there he did not need witnesses'. It was burnt in Danish raids of 1004 and 1010, but its growth continued through much of the 11th century, although a rapid decline had set in by

30 *Viking stirrup from Kilverstone.*

1086. The reasons for this are obscure. It was certainly suffering from the competition of Bury St Edmunds, and probably the newer, larger ships could not negotiate the river Thet.

The story of Norwich, however, was one of continuous growth. It was probably in the Danish period that it developed from a collection of hamlets to a market centre. Certainly between 880 and 920 a market was set up in the Tombland-Cathedral Close area. The town of *Northwic* was enclosed by a bank and ditch, preserved today in the street pattern. A second settlement to the north in the Cowgate-Whitefriars area, called *Needham*, was also enclosed by a ditch. Excavations have produced pottery and millstones from the Midlands as well as much pottery from the Rhineland and northern France. By 1066 *Northwic* had expanded to link with *Westwic* by buildings along St Benedict's Street. By 1086 there were 40 churches and chapels.

The foundation of Yarmouth was probably later than that of Norwich or Thetford. Excavations in the Fullers Hill area, traditionally the first occupied, found no conclusive evidence for settlement before 1000. The archaeo-logical evidence suggested no more than tents, lived in seasonally by visiting fishermen. In 1086 Domesday Book listed 24 fishermen as living in Yarmouth, the only ones mentioned in Norfolk.

31 *The Saxo-Norman tower of St Mary Coslany, Norwich.*

The pre-Conquest period saw the emergence of Norfolk as one of the most populous and wealthy counties in England. However, the Danish threat was never far away. In 993 Norwich and Thetford were sacked, and from 1016 to 1042 England was under the rule of the Danish king Cnut and his sons. In spite of this period of Danish control, the church organisation never broke down completely as previously, probably because the Danes were now Christians. The North Elmham see was revived by 955 and a cathedral built there in the 10th or 11th century it is unclear whether any of this early building survives. In 1071 the see was transferred to Thetford. Although no parish churches can be dated prior to the 11th century, there are some fine examples of late Saxon architecture: over forty churches with identifiable Saxon features remain, scattered all over the

32 *East belfry window, East Lexham church.*

county. The most usual remaining feature is the tower, often round as at East Lexham. A rare example of Saxon decorative mouldings can be seen on the west door and the capitals of the internal arches at Great Dunham. Two crosses survive, one in Whissonsett church, and one from St Vedast's church, now in the Castle Museum.

We know little about daily life and housing, except what we can glean from the Saxon houses excavated at Thetford and North Elmham. At the latter small rectangular houses, with outbuildings and fences between the properties, give us some idea of the group of smallholdings which made up a late Saxon village.

When William the Conqueror had established himself as ruler of England, he wanted to know the extent of his new possessions; he sent out commissioners to collect information which was gathered together to form the Domesday Book of 1086. For Norfolk 731 settlements are mentioned, most of which still exist. The most populated areas were around Norwich and along the east coast, with the breckland and fenland as the most sparsely inhabited districts. The population had shifted since Roman times, when the west of the county had been the most important area. The large flocks of sheep noted in Domesday suggest that Norfolk's medieval prosperity as a farming and wool-producing county was already well-established.

33 Right. *Saxon cross, Whissonsett church.*

34 Far right. *Saxo-Norman tower, Tasburgh church.*

3

Medieval Norfolk

Although life went on after the Norman Conquest much as it had done before, there were very significant changes which eventually affected the lives of all. The feudal system now became central to the workings of government. Of prime importance were the tenants-in-chief within each county. These were the great Norman barons who had come with William and fought at the battle of Hastings, and who in return were granted lands confiscated from Anglo-Saxon lords. There were about 60 holding land from the king in Norfolk, eight of whom were bishops or abbots holding land for their cathedrals or abbeys.

The king also held land directly and was in fact the largest landholder in Norfolk, with estates in 170 parishes. The two major lay tenants-in-chief were William de Warenne and Roger Bigot, both of whom held land in more than 100 parishes. Ecclesiastical tenants held land in over 200 parishes. About 20 tenants had estates in fewer than 20 parishes. Not all tenants-in-chief were noblemen: Edric, holding land in only one parish, was described as a falconer. The only area where this new system of landholding does not seem to have applied was in the broadland region where about 20 'freemen' holding land in their own right are listed.

Most tenants-in-chief held their land scattered about the country rather than in one area, and some of the estates they could not look after themselves were in the hands of bailiffs. Others would have been held on their behalf by local lords who would give feudal military service in return. At the bottom of the social ladder was the serf, who held no land and had to serve his lord.

The east coast, especially the area of the Fleggs, stood out as a distinctive region in Domesday Book. Population was two or three times as high as in the west and farming was intensive, involving the keeping of large flocks of sheep, presumably on the marshes. Abundant meadows are described which must have been in the low-lying area which later became the Broads. Salt-making was also an important industry. To the south, the boulder clays were more densely populated than the loams, sands and gravels to the north. Settlement in the fens was limited to islands in the peat, as at Hilgay and Southery.

The origin of 'hundreds' is not clear, but they certainly existed in the 10th century, and were an essential part of the administration of the Anglo-Saxon kingdom which were carried on by the Normans. They

35 *The 15th-century tower of Salle church.*

36 *Bishops' gate in Norwich, demolished 1791.*

may have been organised originally for fiscal purposes as the area from which the amount of tax or services which was reckoned to be due from 100 hides, was collected. Their actual size varies and often they have natural features or ancient earthworks as their boundaries. Local government was carried out by local meetings held usually in the open air, where thieves would be brought to justice, disputes settled and stray cattle rounded up. The meeting place in Forehoe Hundred, for instance, was at a group of four barrows or 'hoes' in the parish of Forehoe. The 38 hundreds remained a very important division until the 1960s, only finally losing their administrative significance with the reorganisation of local government in 1974.

The towns

Of the three major towns of medieval Norfolk, Lynn, Yarmouth and Norwich, the last is the only one with substantial Anglo-Saxon origins. The steady growth of its trade and population on a very favourable site suffered a temporary setback with the Norman invasion: the number of burgesses fell from 1,320 in 1066 to 665 in 1086. Meanwhile the Normans were establishing their own zones. Their borough was in the St Peter Mancroft area, and provided a new focus away from the old one round Tombland, and the new market place superseded the older site. More important for the domination of the region in the early Norman period was the castle. A hundred houses in the heart of the old Anglo-Saxon town were destroyed to make room for it. The first castle, built shortly after the Conquest, was probably of wood on a mound or motte; but this was replaced between 1120 and 1130 by a stone keep, the only royal castle in Norfolk or Suffolk.

This initial destruction of property was followed by a second catastrophe when in 1075 following Earl Ralf's rebellion against William, houses were burnt down during the disturbances. Finally, when the cathedral was begun in 1096 more houses and at least two churches were destroyed to create a large precinct. Within 50 years of the Conquest, the Normans did more to alter the layout of Norwich than their successors over the next 500 years. The ruthless destruction of property and the establishment of privileged communities of foreign monks and merchants within their walls must have been hateful to the English inhabitants.

There were many more castles across the county, some being among the finest Norman examples in England. William de Warenne fortified Castle Acre where his earthworks enclose 15 acres. New Buckenham and Castle Rising were built in the mid-12th century by William d'Albini. Castle Rising is one of the most ornate keeps in England, and New Buckenham's circular version is one of the earliest examples of its type. Sometimes the Normans re-used old defensive sites. Thetford, with the highest motte in the county, was within an Iron Age fort, while Burgh Castle now levelled, was sited on the old Roman shore fort. Not all castles were built immediately following the Conquest. There were several later periods of unrest which encouraged castle-building. Bishop

I *Scolt Head, off the north Norfolk coast, now owned by the National Trust.*

II *Hunstanton, Victorian seaside resort on top of the cliffs.*

III *Castle Acre Castle with its planned town within ramparts beside it.*

IV *Thetford Priory ruins from the air.*

37 *Motte and bailey castle at Middleton Mount, near King's Lynn, reconstruction drawing by Sue White.*

38 *West front, Castle Acre priory.*

39 *Late-medieval houses in the main street, Little Walsingham.*

Despenser's castle at North Elmham was built during the period of peasa. rebellion in the 1380s, and the 15th-century Wars of the Roses sa many fortified constructions appearing, amongst them those at Gresha and Caistor, homes of the Paston family, famous for the large numb of their surviving letters.

The Normans did not only build castles, but also churches. In 10⁷ Herfast, Bishop of Elmham, transferred his see to Thetford, and h successor, Herbert de Losinga, took the decision to move it again, Norwich. He was one of the most accomplished and cultured bishops his time; the most important of his many contributions to Norman chur architecture was the new cathedral in Norwich. The foundation sto⟩ was laid in 1096 and it took 50 years to build. Attached to it was Benedictine priory of 60 monks. Losinga's enthusiasm—he found St Nicholas's in Yarmouth and St Margaret's in King's Lynn as well the cathedral—inspired others, and the 28 years of his bishopric saw t construction of many Norfolk churches.

As the population grew in the 12th and 13th centuries, a new for of village layout, sometimes at a distance from the original settleme near the church, began to appear. This was the 'green village' where t farmsteads were placed around a green or common kept as permane pasture. Some villages had more than one green. Several large a⟩

impressive examples survive, as at Hales, Mulbarton and Brisley. It is difficult to say why they became important from the 12th century, but possibly as more areas of woodland and waste were brought into cultivation, it was necessary to preserve some pasture near the centre of the settlement.

Small market towns grew up, scattered fairly evenly over the more fertile areas between eight and 10 miles apart. This meant that no farmer or village craftsman would have to walk more than four or five miles to sell his goods. The prosperity of these little towns is suggested by the size of their market places and the grandeur of their churches. Not all these towns grew up naturally; some were created by manorial lords hoping to make profits from their markets. Some of these speculations were successful, some were not. Both Castle Rising and New Buckenham were founded by the powerful William d'Albini alongside his castles. The most successful venture was the Bishop of Norwich's creation at Lynn.

The earliest settlement at Lynn may have been around All Saints Church in South Lynn, on a consolidated sand bank to the west of a dyke that kept the sea from the low-lying land of Hardwick and Gaywood. The name probably derives from the British/Welsh word 'llyn' meaning 'pool or lake'. Although the original settlement would have been primarily agricultural, the production of salt was no doubt also important. It was not until the 13th century that the outlet of the Ouse at Wisbech silted up and instead the river found its way to the sea at Lynn, greatly increasing Lynn's waterborne trade routes. Even before this, however, the town had had good communications, and it was this that Bishop Losinga hoped to exploit when he granted a market and fair to St Margaret's Church and Priory in 1095.

This stimulated the development of a new settlement at Lynn between Millfleet and Purfleet, in a half mile stretch of marsh running

40 *Medieval King's Lynn.*

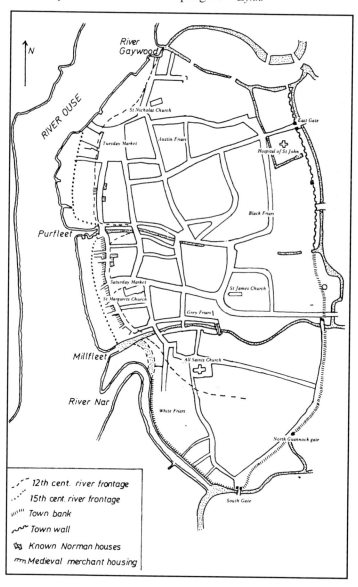

12th cent. river frontage
15th cent. river frontage
Town bank
Town wall
Known Norman houses
Medieval merchant housing

41 Left. *Trinity Guildhall, King's Lynn.*

42 Below left. *Market house in the market place of the planned town of New Buckenham. Built in 1559, the upper floor was replaced in the 18th century. The market and town courts were held in the upper room and the whipping post can still be seen.*

43 Below right. *Wymondham market house was built in 1618 to replace that burnt down in the town fire of 1615. The upper room was used by the market clerk and the town council.*

back to the sea-bank at Guannock. It flourished and expanded to the east very rapidly. Within 50 years the town had outgrown its original site, and between 1146 and 1179 the Bishops of Norwich established a new market to serve a second community, together with St Nicholas's Church. This settlement remained under the direct control of the bishopric, and it was not until 1204 that the two sites were united as Bishop's Lynn. The original Lynn, at South Lynn, was administered separately until 1555.

Throughout the Middle Ages, the river line of the Ouse was being pushed westwards. Slowly the area west of St Margaret's was reclaimed and built up with warehouses and rich merchants' houses of which Hampton Court and Clifton House are fine examples. The richest members of the community were the merchants, who lived near the quays, in houses along King Street, Queen Street, St Margaret's Place, Nelson Street and Bridge Street. Their houses fronted onto the street with yards, warehouses and cellars stretching back to the river behind.

At first sight, the line of the Lynn defences appears to enclose a surprisingly large area. However, they do in fact follow the line of the natural old sea-banks, probably the edge of the lake on whose shores Lynn was sited. The defences were mostly in the form of an earthwork. The Eastgate was probably built between 1327 and 1377 and the present Southgate is a late medieval structure. The North Guannock gate is perhaps the oldest surviving one, partly dating from the late 13th century.

Lynn has been described as a 'mushroom town' of the early Middle Ages. Grain was one of its major exports, especially to Norway. From the 12th century onwards, wool was in even greater demand on the Continent than corn, and this became Lynn's most important export. Salt also remained an important part of its trade. Merchants exchanged their goods for a variety of foreign luxuries: wine came from Gascony and fish from North Germany and the Baltic, from whence also came two more valuable imports—timber and furs. Spanish traders were also to be found in Lynn, bringing with them raisins, figs, dates and leather from Cordova. King John's Custom which was a list drawn up covering most English ports between 1203-5, shows that after London and Southampton, Lynn and Boston were the most prosperous ports in England.

Trade was increasing throughout the period, and the prosperity of Norwich with it. Its importance is shown by the fact that there were five bridges across the river—more than in any other English medieval town. In 1334, Norwich was the sixth richest town in England, with a population of about 6,000. Particularly in the area around the market, the citizens became more and more cramped along narrow lanes. The market had extended beyond its original site; horses were sold in Rampant Horse Street, swine on Orford Hill and All Saints Green. Cattle, sheep, poultry and cheese were sold in the square south of St Peter Mancroft. The main market was unusual in being held daily, and it is still the largest open market in England. By 1397 it was dominated as today by stalls providing provisions for the city.

44 *Merchants' marks from King's Lynn.*

45 *Tombland Alley, Norwich.*

Norwich was frequently held or attacked by rebels in the early Middle Ages, the most serious occasion being in 1217 when the city was invaded by Prince Louis of France who took control of the castle and laid the town waste. It is not surprising that by the second half of the 13th century much of the city was surrounded by a bank. The city wall was built between 1297 and 1334. It encloses a very large area, much of which remained open ground until after the end of the Middle Ages.

The lack of respect felt for many of the bishops and priors of Norwich, many of whom were royal servants with little interest in their ecclesiastical duties, was reflected in the frequent disputes that broke out between the city and the priory of Norwich. It was almost inevitable that during the period when the corporation was increasing its control over civic life it would cast jealous eyes towards the very large areas of ecclesiastical land beyond its influence. At the time of the Trinity Fair in 1272 the bad feeling between town and clergy led to a full-scale attack on the priory. To compensate for the destruction wrought, the citizens had to erect St Ethelbert's gate and the monks were given control of Bishop's Bridge. Despite these internal problems, Norwich's wealth and influence continued to increase throughout the medieval period.

Yarmouth, on a sand bank at the mouth of the river Yare, owes its existence to the arrival, each autumn, of vast shoals of herring off the coast. The settlement probably began as a seasonal camping-site where fishermen could pull up their boats and dry their nets. Gradually it became more permanent, so that by 1086 there was a small borough of about 400 people. Possibly as the sand spit changed its form and the northern outlet of the Yare began to silt up, the settlement moved south so that by the end of the 11th century, when St Nicholas's was founded, it was centred on its present site.

Its position on a sand bank, recently emerged from the sea, meant that it was royal property. The site was restricted and useless for cultivation. The sand hills on the seaward side, known as the Denes, were used for pasture and net drying. By 1277, windmills had been erected there, and the Denes were also the venue for the annual fish fair.

French, Dutch, Scandinavian and even Italian boats came to fish off Yarmouth. This buying and selling developed into one of the greatest medieval fairs of Europe and lasted from Michaelmas to Martinmas. The importance of herring to Yarmouth is shown by the inclusion of three herring in the coat of arms adopted when the town was granted a charter in 1209. Other industries grew up to serve the fish trade, including herring curing and salt making. It is not clear how important the herring smoking industry was, but there are references to 'fish houses' and contracts for curing herring from the mid-13th century. The herring fairs reached their peak in the 13th and early 14th centuries, when in one season 300 ships paid tolls at Yarmouth.

Yarmouth was important to the defence of the eastern counties, and in 1260 permission to enclose the town with a wall and moat was granted. It was completed about 1485, and contained eight gates and about 15 towers. No-one was allowed to live outside the town walls, and the very restricted nature of the site resulted in a congested layout with characteristic 'Rows': narrow alleys running east to west from the market place to the harbour. The narrowest was only 27 inches wide at one point; special little carts were developed for use there.

46 *Great Yarmouth coat of arms, granted in 1340.*

The Church

The prosperity of early medieval Norfolk was not only reflected in its expanding towns, but throughout the countryside, principally in the churches. Norfolk has more medieval churches than any other county of comparable size, many of which are very large and fine examples. It is clear that laymen contributed generously to their building. The finest example of a Norfolk Norman church is at Hales. A similar church with carvings probably by the same mason survives at nearby Heckingham. Early Norman sculpture is rare in Norfolk as elsewhere, but a very fine example, of a seated figure with raised arms may be seen over the south doorway of Haddiscoe church. Examples of 13th-century, or Early English, church architecture, are more difficult to find, but in the fens, at Walsoken and Tilney All Saints and above all at West Walton, there are some good specimens.

The number of religious houses founded in Norfolk also demonstrates the county's wealth. A minimum of 150 religious houses, including five nunneries were established, and substantial remains survive on about fifty sites. The first Benedictine monastery in Norfolk to be founded after the Viking raids was St Benet's Abbey, re-established by King Cnut in 1016 on a remote and marshy site in what is now the Norfolk Broads. The next and by far the most important Benedictine house was that attached to Norwich Cathedral. Priories were founded by Bishop Losinga in Lynn and Yarmouth when he built churches there.

There was much Cluniac influence from the Continent after the Norman Conquest, and the first Cluniac house in Norfolk was built at Castle Acre by William de Warenne. Two other important Cluniac houses were founded in Norfolk—one at Bromholm, and one at Thetford.

47 *Adam Cutlawe, Chaplain, West Lynn, 1503.*

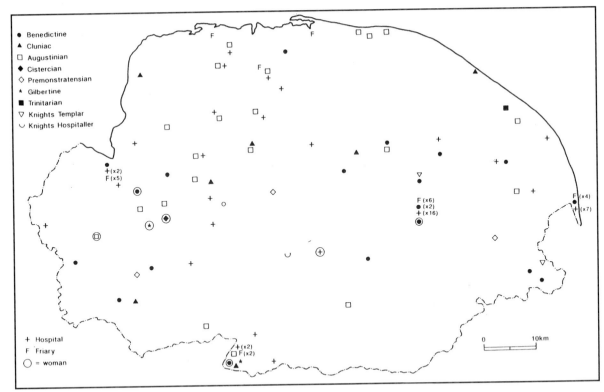

Benedictine
Cluniac
Augustinian
Cistercian
Premonstratensian
Gilbertine
Trinitarian
Knights Templar
Knights Hospitaller

+ Hospital
F Friary
○ = woman

48 Above. *Monasteries in medieval Norfolk.*

49 Left. *Stained glass panel, Tottington, 1340-60.*

The only purely English order was founded by St Gilbert of Sempringham in 1131 and was unusual in that 'double monasteries' were set up for men and women. Stores, money and books were controlled by the nuns, the management of property and buying and selling by the monks. The only one founded in Norfolk was at Shouldham at the beginning of the 13th century.

The Knights Hospitaller of St John of Jerusalem were an entirely different type of monastic order. They had become a regular standing army defending Jerusalem, and also provided medical services. The Order also contained nursing sisters. Before 1180 there was a small nunnery of the Order at Carbrooke, near Watton, and in 1193 further lands there were granted and a monastery or 'commandery' was founded. The Hospitallers undertook military exercises rather than manual work like other monastic orders and collected money for the Order's overseas activities.

Canons, who lived a regular communal life without taking a vow of poverty whilst performing the duties of parish priests, were distinct from monks. The earliest order was that of the Austin or Black Canons, while in 1121 the reforming Premonstratensian order was founded with stricter regulations. About twenty-two houses of Austin Canons were established in Norfolk in the 12th and early 13th centuries. Some, such as those at Beeston and Hempton were small and that at North Creake began as a small hospital, but the largest and richest house was that at the shrine of Walsingham. The Trinitarian Canons were an unusual order, particularly concerned with the fate of captives. They founded only 12 houses in England, that at Ingham being the last to be established, in 1360.

50 *Stained glass roundel from Ringland, 1466.*

By the early 13th century there was a feeling that even the newest orders were becoming very wealthy and no longer exhibited the poverty and humility expected of them. To overcome this, orders of friars were founded. They renounced the corporate ownership of property and instead were to stay in lodgings and live off charity. Rather than withdrawing from the world, they went into towns to teach and preach. There were four main orders, all to be found in Norfolk. The Dominicans, or Black Friars, were founded in France in 1216 and had friaries in Lynn, Norwich, Yarmouth and Thetford. The Franciscans, or Grey Friars, were founded in 1223 and reached Norwich and Yarmouth in 1226. They also set up a friary at Walsingham in 1347. The Carmelites, or White Friars, began as hermits who were forced to leave Palestine in 1240. The following year they established their first Norfolk friary at Burnham Norton, but did not settle in Norwich until 1257. By the end of the century they had friaries in Blakeney, Lynn and Yarmouth. The Austin Friars arrived in 1249 and soon had friaries in Lynn, Norwich, Yarmouth and Thetford.

The obvious poverty and dedication of these orders attracted support and donations, which meant that they too were soon erecting fine buildings, and soon they became as wealthy as the earlier orders. Unlike other orders they owned no land except that on which their buildings stood. Very few friary buildings have survived, because their location in town centres meant that at the Reformation their new owners demolished them for the value of their sites. St Andrew's Hall in Norwich is the only friars' church in England to have survived almost in its entirety.

Pious laymen who could not afford to found a monastery sometimes undertook the establishment of 'hospitals' instead. Some, such as the one on the Norwich to Walsingham road at Billingford, were to shelter pilgrims, while others, like that at Yarmouth, were to provide a home for the poor. Some were specifically for the sick, often for lepers. Norwich had six leper houses, Lynn five, Thetford four and Yarmouth two. The most famous of all Norfolk hospitals and one which survives today was the Great Hospital of St Giles, founded in 1249 by Bishop Walter Suffield near the cathedral. Although many monasteries, friaries and hospitals have disappeared without trace, it is clear that Norfolk could boast some very impressive architecture and well-endowed religious houses worthy of the wealthiest corner of medieval England.

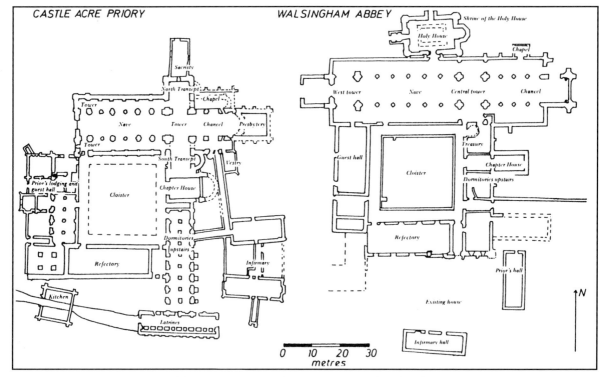

51 *Norfolk monasteries: Castle Acre priory and Walsingham abbey.*

52 *The Great Hospital in Norwich.*

Agriculture

Farming and landholding in the Middle Ages were mostly based on the manor house, the owner of which had financial and judicial control over the villagers. All land transactions took place at the manor court, and the system whereby peasants held land in exchange for a combination of rent and labour services was organised from there. As well as the peasant holdings there was demesne land, which was farmed directly by the lord with the help of the peasantry's labour services. The area of manorial jurisdiction did not necessarily coincide with that of a village. More usually a single manor had rights within several villages, and often a village owed duty to several different lords. In 1316 Fincham had five lords and Sall seven, while some had as many as eighteen.

During the 12th century waste land was being taken into cultivation all over the county and woods being felled. By the end of the century there was very little spare land left, and the ever-increasing population had to be fed by more intensive agriculture. Complex rotations were practised and the traditional fallow year replaced by a crop of legumes which used the field while replacing nitrogen into the soil. The destruction of woodland made it necessary for other sources of fuel to be exploited, of which peat, dug from the area now covered by the Broads, was one of the most important. However, by the 1340s the peat was becoming more difficult to extract, and the areas of old diggings flooded. Slowly the Broads were being formed.

53 Prior's lodging, Castle Acre Priory, watercolour by David Yaxley, 1980.

*54 Windmill,
Weasenham St Peter,
c.1590.*

We can see a glimpse of a 'typical' manor at Forncett, where about a fifth of the land was farmed by the lord—just over 300 acres—and by the late 13th century, less than a third of the land was fallow. Barley was the principal crop, but yields were small possibly because of over-intensive farming. Both horses and oxen were kept as draught animals. Some calves were sold while others were kept for home consumption. Manure spreading was important, and was one of the duties tenants owed to the demesne farm.

The intense degree of subdivision of landholdings shows how great was the pressure on the available land. In Martham by the mid-14th century the average size of holding was under three acres. This picture of intensive farming by a numerous peasantry with small holdings changes abruptly after the first half of the 14th century. It is generally accepted that the climate was deteriorating and brought with it bad harvests and starvation. Land which had been forced to produce increasing yields over several centuries became exhausted; an undernourished population had less resistance to disease. The Black Death reached Norfolk in 1349 and large numbers of people died. Subsequent outbreaks of plague were responsible for a continuing population decline, into the early 16th century and affected daily life in many ways.

Mortality was probably greatest in the first outbreak of 1349; over 200 new clerical appointments had to be made, for instance. It is not surprising to find that in 1368 many churches in the Archdeaconry of Norwich were already ruinous or united with others. Norwich was hit by plague in 1361-2 and 1369, as well as in 1349. It may well have lost two-fifths of its population and half its clergy. However, by 1400 the city had recovered its prosperity. Other smaller towns were not so fortunate. By 1334 Yarmouth had become one of the largest provincial towns, but the Black Death reduced its population from about 10,000 to less than 3,000. At villages such as Litcham and Foulsham surviving market places suggest the lost prosperity of the 13th century, which has never returned.

The late 14th century was a time of unrest in the countryside as feudal society was giving way to an economy based on wages and rent. The culmination of this unrest was the Peasants' Revolt of 1381, the immediate cause of which was the imposition of an unpopular poll tax. There was widespread unrest in Norfolk, concentrated on two weeks in the middle of June and a principal target for the insurgents was the residence of John Reed, a collector of poll tax at Rougham, although manor court rolls were destroyed in many houses across the county. The rebellion was put down by the local gentry under the leadership of Bishop Despenser of Norwich. The final confrontation took place in June near North Walsham when the rebels' leader, Geoffrey Litster, was summarily executed. Rebellion was put down.

55 Stained glass roundel from Coslany church, Norwich, showing a man sowing seed, 1480-1500.

As there were fewer people trying to make a living in the country-side, the size of landholdings could increase. By 1497 the average for Martham was 9.3 acres. The peasant smallholder was being replaced by

relatively substantial tenant farmers. In Hemsby 16 individuals held nearly 80 per cent of the land in 1500, while in 1454 in Elmham 59 per cent of the arable land was held by 12 large tenants. Late medieval tenants were not only fewer in number and farming larger holdings, but the terms on which they held their land had also changed. Labour services were becoming less common, leases were longer and the rent fixed for longer periods. With the virtual end of labour services, it was no longer worthwhile for manorial lords to farm their demesne directly, and at Forncett after 1376 it was let. The manorial farm buildings became derelict and by 1490 the manor house itself had gone.

56   The 15th-century barn at Hales Hall, Loddon.

A further indication of the declining population in the late Middle Ages is the large number of deserted and shrunken villages. Forty per cent of early medieval sites in the Hundred of Launditch have been abandoned; many of these were settlements on marginal land, founded when farming was at its most intensive. It is only rarely possible to date the desertion of villages, but none seem to have been abandoned as a direct result of the Black Death—indeed, most desertions do not seem to have occurred until about 100 years later. A smaller population needed less food, and so there was not the same market for cereal crops, while the demand for English wool was constantly increasing. Both the new group of tenant farmers and the lords who chose to continue farming their demesnes began to keep more sheep, and this led to the enclosure of land for the purpose. This process contributed to the decline in the numbers of small farmers. It is certainly possible that some 16th-century

57 *Aerial view of Pudding Norton deserted village, showing the street curving through the middle, and rectangular tofts on either side.*

58 *Romanesque font at Burnham Deepdale church showing the autumn tasks of threshing with a flail.*

desertions were the result of oppression, as landlords strove to obtain control of all the common lands for sheep pasture. However, it is far more likely that in villages initially reduced in population by the Black Death, where decline continued, landlords eventually moved in when there were too few inhabitants left to make effective protests.

This shift in emphasis to wool production meant new prosperity for some social groups, most obviously for the wool producers and merchants. Evidence of their wealth can be seen in fine manor houses all over the county, and in the great 'wool churches'. Perhaps less obvious was the benefit the wool trade brought to the many peasants and cottagers who spun wool and wove cloth. In 1329 worsted cloth was being produced in the parishes of Sloley, Dilham, Walsham, Tunstead, Honing, Scottow and Catton, as well as the towns of Aylsham and Worsted, from which the cloth took its name. This marks the transition from small-scale subsistence farming to production for a market, which we associate with the shift from a medieval to a modern economy.

59 *Carved angel from the double hammer-beam roof at Knapton, 1504.*

The later Middle Ages

Partly because of the wealth produced by the cloth trade, there was a great flowering of church architecture in Norfolk from the 14th century onwards, during the periods when the Decorated and Perpendicular styles were at their best. The most elaborate churches are to be found in the wealthiest areas—for instance, the fens. At Terrington, Walpole St Peter, Walsoken and West Walton, the churches are of cathedral-like proportions and among the finest in the county. Other impressive buildings are to be found in the medieval ports, especially on the north coast. The churches of Cley, Brancaster, and Wiveton, as well as the east coast village of Winterton, show something of Norfolk's medieval prosperity. Individual patrons might pay for the erection of a new tower or porch and this resulted in some quite humble churches with lavish additions, such as the splendid porch at Pulham St Mary, built in the 15th century.

Another way in which the wealthy could display their religious convictions was to leave money for the setting up of a chantry chapel, supplied with a priest to pray for their soul; many parish churches, such as Outwell, were extended in the 15th century for this purpose. An extremely well-off patron might be able to create a 'college', to which the whole church would be appropriated, and arrange for its administration by chaplains, as at Thompson and Attleborough.

It is in the carving on ceilings, screens and bench ends that the work of 15th-century Norfolk woodcarvers can be seen at its best. Over 200 screens survive, although most give only a slight impression of their original appearance. Usually they had a walkway along the top where choir boys sang. The screens at Ranworth and Attleborough are unique in that this walkway has been preserved. The fine hammerbeam and double hammerbeam roofs of many Norfolk churches also date from the 15th century. Beautiful 'angel' roofs survive at Cawston, Swaffham and Necton. The bench ends at Tuttington are particularly attractive.

60 *Bench end in Tuttington church.*

61 *Margery Kempe, 1373-1440.*

The 14th century was the great age of mysticism and the English recluse or anchorite: someone, not necessarily in religious orders, who chose to retreat from the world for prayer and meditation. One of the most famous was Julian of Norwich who lived from about 1373 to 1416 in an anchorage attached to the church of St Julian and St Edward, Conisford. She became an anchorite as a result of divine revelations received whilst suffering from a serious illness. In her cell she wrote her fine mystical work *Revelations of Divine Love*. She wrote in English, perhaps because she did not know enough Latin, and shows herself through her writings to have been a sympathetic, shrewd and learned person.

Another way in which the religious revival of the 14th century was demonstrated was in the great increase in the popularity of pilgrimages. There were many shrines in Norfolk, but the most popular was at Walsingham. Its origins are obscure. It probably began as a place of private devotion built about 1130 by a wealthy widow as a replica of the house at Nazareth where the Annunciation took place. By the 13th century, however, it was the statue of Our Lady that was the chief object of veneration. From 1226, the shrine was regularly visited by royalty, and by 1290 it had acquired national importance. The Slipper Chapel at Houghton St Giles was built in the mid-14th century. Here pilgrims would leave their shoes and go the rest of the way to Walsingham barefoot. Many bought pilgrim badges as souvenirs, which are found all over England. All types of people went there, from fishermen of Winterton who had lost their nets, to gaolbirds escaping the law, all seeking divine aid.

Religion was not something just for special occasions like pilgrimages, however, but a part of daily life. All the trade guilds had their own chapels. Guild plays, always with a religious theme, were being performed in Norwich by the 15th century. The mercers and drapers performed 'The Creation of the World' and the grocers and tallow chandlers produced 'Paradise'.

The late 14th century saw the beginning of a decline in the trade and commercial importance of both Lynn and Yarmouth. Wars with France meant that the wine trade contracted, and changes in fashion caused a decline in the export of wool and import of fur. Instead of exporting raw wool, England now concentrated on finished cloth, but this tended to go through Norwich, and to a lesser extent, Yarmouth rather than Lynn. The most significant reason for the decline of the latter, however, was the increased power of the North German ports of the Hanseatic League, which prevented any trade with the Baltic area apart from their own. Norwegian ships disappeared from Lynn and were replaced by German ones. The League built its own warehouse, the 'Steel Yard', in Lynn. Within their own district they lived as a tight community under their own laws. The Hanseatic control was so frustrating for Lynn merchants that in the early 15th century they attempted to break the embargo and sail to Iceland with cargoes of malt, cloth and hardware; but such was the power of the League that this was forbidden in 1426. Lynn was, therefore, out of the mainstream of England's

62 *Thomas Elys, a rich merchant of Norwich, and his wife Margaret.*

63 *Fenland churches: Walpole St Peter.*

64 *Fenland churches: Terrinton St Clement.*

65 *Pilgrim badge showing Our Lady of Walsingham.*

international trade by the 15th century, but her hinterland was still prosperous, and provided a market for a great variety of imports. Lynn was still relatively well off, as shown by the number of fine late medieval buildings in the town. However, by the early 16th century this spate of building was over, and instead much property became derelict. Coastal trade alone remained important.

After 1360 there was a decline in the number of fish sold at Yarmouth, and by the 15th century most were in fact being caught by Dutchmen. The decline of the English fishing fleet was a matter of grave concern to the government, which relied on merchant vessels for its navy in time of war. One problem which dogged Yarmouth throughout the later Middle Ages was that of keeping the entrance to the harbour on the Yare open. The sandbank on which Yarmouth stood was growing across the estuary, and by 1336 the town was without a navigable haven. Six attempts were made between 1340 and 1560 to dig a new entrance, but it was not until 1560 that a satisfactory cut was constructed, which has lasted with little alteration till today.

In the 14th century, three-quarters of the worsted cloth exported from England went through Yarmouth. The great variety of Continental pottery excavated there shows the town's far-flung trading links. However, the problems posed by the harbour entrance, and the reduction of population following the Black Death, meant that the port declined in the second half of the century, and many sites within it were abandoned.

Unlike Lynn and Yarmouth, the wealth of Norwich increased without interruption. By 1400 it had become the chief centre for worsted manufacture. The trade was regulated by a small group of merchants controlling powerful trade guilds. These men became immensely rich and formed a dominating oligarchy. Most of the weavers were craftsmen working on a small scale, and their total exclusion from the administration of the city and the industry aroused their resentment. In the 16th century many of them were to support Kett's unsuccessful rebellion. Nevertheless, despite these social tensions, at the beginning of the 16th century Norwich was without doubt the leading urban and commercial centre in the county.

4

Church and State

The 16th and 17th centuries saw many dramatic developments in men's ideas about the nature of true religion, and of right government. Norfolk did not escape involvement in these great national changes. Protestantism took root early in the county, and Norfolk men and women were not afraid to fight for their beliefs in matters of church or state. Contemporaries described the typical Norfolk man as dour, stubborn and fond of argument, all of which may have contributed to the development of what were to become known as 'puritanical' views by the 17th century.

66 Far left. *John Deynes, mariner, from a brass at Beeston Regis church, 1527. Note the mariner's whistle.*

67 Left. *Wife of John Deynes, from a brass in Beeston Regis church, 1527.*

In the late 14th century the movement known as Lollardy had appeared. Lollards wanted more freedom of religious thought, and particularly sought the right to interpret the Bible for themselves. Their leader, John Wycliffe, supported the translation of the Bible into English. Bishop Despenser, who became Bishop of Norwich in 1370, was notorious for his hatred of Lollardy, and the first burnings for heresy in the city took place on his instructions. The first Lollard to be burnt was William Sawtre, priest of St Margaret's, Lynn.

Although the Lollards were driven underground in the 15th century, a new wave of criticism of the Roman Catholic church began in the early 16th century. English Bibles, and later the writings of Martin Luther, were smuggled into the country, and burnings of Norfolk Lollards continued into the 16th century. One of the most famous was Thomas Bilney, who was burnt in the 'Lollards' pit' in Norwich in 1531, shortly before the final break with Rome.

68 *The 15th-century flint and stone work at St Michael at Coslany, Norwich.*

Despite this tradition of radical dissent from the established church, there were conspiracies against the dissolution of the Norfolk monasteries. If it had not been for the vigilance of the Dukes of Norfolk and Suffolk, there might well have been risings on the scale of those in Yorkshire. However, motives for discontent were not entirely religious. Very few clerics were involved; instead it was men like the innkeepers round Walsingham who protested, fearing loss of trade with the closure of the shrine. Many of the poor realised that church lands would soon find their way into the hands of the gentry whom they regarded as their oppressors. One conspirator urged that all the gentlemen should be killed, while another, George Gysbergh of Walsingham, who was later hanged, said that he thought it 'very ill done, the suppressing of so many religious houses where God was well served'.

It was not until the reign of Edward VI that the effects of the reformation begun under Henry VIII were felt at local level. Between 1549 and 1551, church interiors had to be altered to suit a simpler form of service: for instance, altars had to be moved forward into the choir and any wall-paintings whitewashed over. From the churchwardens' accounts of North Elmham all these changes can be followed:

Item - myself ... one day pulling down the said altars - 18d.
Item - To Richard Tilney for casting and whitening the wall where the high altar was before - 4d.

Mary's accession in 1553 meant that England became, temporarily, a Catholic country again. This was very unpopular in Norfolk, where many men and women were burnt as heretics in Norwich—more than any other dioceses except London and Canterbury.

After five years Mary was succeeded by her half-sister Elizabeth, who, though herself a Protestant, was determined to keep to a middle way in religious matters. She steered a course between specifically Catholic practices and the demands of the Protestant radicals, who were becoming known as 'puritans' and demanded a Presbyterian system of church government. Elizabeth's first archbishop, Matthew Parker, was the son of a Norwich merchant. He was an excellent administrator who was in sympathy with most of the Queen's views and did his best to produce a Church of England which avoided any extremes. However, puritanism gained ground in Norfolk, a tendency encouraged by the many Protestant refugees who fled there from persecution in France and the Low Countries. Support for puritanism was at its strongest in the towns.

The real clash over religion came after 1633 when Archbishop Laud was appointed and began to enforce High Church policies. In 1635 Matthew Wren, an ardent supporter of his, became Bishop of Norwich. His enthusiasm for enforcing uniformity drove many Norfolk puritans to seek refuge in Holland; perhaps as many as 3,000 left.

The royal government's patronage of Laud and his followers did much to discredit it in the eyes of many, and probably contributed to the decision of many Norfolk men to support Parliament during the Civil War. While the war was being fought, Parliament passed laws intended to make England a puritan country, removing 'pagan' decorations and ornaments from churches, and abolishing bishops in 1647. The destruction of church ornaments was officially encouraged from 1643, and the attack of the Parliamentary agents on the Cathedral was watched by Bishop Hall, Wren's successor, with horror:

What clattering of glasses! What beating down of walls! What tearing up of monuments! What pulling down of seats! What wresting out of iron and brass from the windows and graves! ... and what a hideous triumph on the market day before all the country when in a kind of sacrilegious and profane procession all the organ pipes, vestments, both copes and surplices, together with the leaden cross which had been newly sawn down from the Green Yard pulpit and the service books and singing books which could be had, were carried to the fire in the public market place.

From Norwich this ferocious destruction spread to the countryside. However, some churches were lucky: St Peter Mancroft in Norwich does not appear to have been desecrated, and the magnificent Ranworth screen with its many portraits of saints is another remarkable survival.

69 *Joseph Hall, Bishop of Norwich.*

70 *Rood screen at Barton Turf church.*

Committees were appointed to examine ministers whose loyalty to Parliament was suspect. They all had to accept the Covenant, which completely renounced any episcopal form of church government, a formula unacceptable to many. Although undoubtedly there were some unworthy Royalist clergymen, others lost their livings for reasons which now seem trivial, like Robert le Neve of Scottow who made a joke at a christening dinner about a pudding which he described as a 'roundhead'. The ejection of these clergy meant that many puritans excluded earlier by Bishop Wren could return, although in many cases their triumph was only temporary: at the Restoration the ejected Royalists generally regained their livings.

Although religious matters helped to polarise opinion before the Civil War, they were neither the sole cause of the war, nor the only issue on which men were divided. Certainly all the Catholic families of Norfolk, such as the Bedingfields at Oxborough, were to support the Royalist cause, but divisions were often found within families. Two of the sons of Chief Justice Coke were Royalist, whilst a third, John Coke of Holkham, was Parliamentarian. Norfolk was a county with no aristocratic leadership or connections at Court, which weakened the possibility of it sympathising with the Royalist cause. The economic policies of the royal government were unpopular and ineffectual, and had no appeal for the hardworking Norfolk yeoman farmers and the gentry who had emerged from the ranks of the yeomanry. The Norfolk centre of the anti-government party was the house of the Hobart family at Blickling, while supporters of the King were found mainly in the north-west, Hamon Le Strange of Hunstanton being one of the most prominent.

Norfolk was fortunate in that when war was finally declared in 1642, most of the action passed her by. The Royalists had most support around Lynn, but everywhere they were outnumbered. The county passed under the control of a Deputy Lieutenant appointed by Parliament, and in December 1642 the counties of Norfolk, Suffolk, Essex, Cambridgeshire, Hertfordshire and the Isle of Ely were linked together for mutual defence in the Eastern Association. It was here that Oliver Cromwell raised the nucleus of the New Model Army which was to play such a major part in the defeat of the Royalists. In 1643 Norfolk raised £60,000 in taxes towards the Parliamentarian war effort; the young people of Norwich collected enough money amongst themselves to equip a troop of cavalry which became known as the 'Maidens' Troop'.

Colonel Cromwell had a shrewd suspicion by March 1643 that the town of Lynn posed a potential threat to Parliament. He wrote that 'I hear they are building a nest there, that we must rifle, I sadly fear'. That summer his suspicions proved justified. A Royalist army under the Duke of Newcastle successfully managed to drive along the east coast, overrunning Lincolnshire and threatening the Eastern Association. This encouraged the Norfolk Royalists to make a stand, and Lynn, under the leadership of Sir Hamon Le Strange, finally declared its support for the king on 13 August. Parliamentary forces, under the Duke of Manchester, blockaded and besieged the town. By September West Lynn was in their hands, which meant that the main town could be bombarded across the river. The daily fighting 'kept the towne in continuall alarme and did so terrifie the people'. They hoped for relief from Newcastle's forces, but he marched no further south than Lincolnshire. In mid-September, after a formal refusal by the town to surrender, Manchester cut its water supply, and slowly the morale of the defenders was worn down. They finally capitulated on 19 September. The leading Royalists were taken prisoner, and Lynn had a Parliamentary garrison for the rest of the war. Once Parliament had established firm control over the whole of England, all those who had supported the king had their estates sequestered (withheld) from them, until they paid large fines. These fines, and the income from the estates gained whilst they were in government hands, went towards the cost of maintaining a standing army.

71 *Chief Justice Coke, 1552-1634.*

72 *Sir Thomas Browne.*

In 1646 King Charles decided that he must escape from his head-quarters at Oxford, where he was in danger of capture by his enemies. At the end of April, disguised as a servant, he arrived in Downham Market where he intended to stay at the *White Swan Inn* to await a message from the Scots, with whom he hoped to make a more favourable agreement than with the English Parliament. Fear of detection made him move to Mundford. As he could not get a boat at Lynn, he moved on via Crimplesham to the Southery ferry, and then went north to Scotland. Six months later he was to be handed over as a prisoner to the English Parliamentary forces by the Scots.

More and more moderates were becoming disaffected with the radical policies which were being forcefully advocated in London, so much so that even in the puritan and parliamentarian city of Norwich there was a riot. Fear that Parliament would interfere with local privileges drove many to support the Royalist cause, and rioting broke out. Cavalry were sent from East Dereham to quell the trouble. The rebels, looking for arms, stormed the headquarters of the county committee. One of the defenders of the building fired from a window and killed a boy. From this moment the trouble escalated and the crowd broke into the building. When the cavalry arrived street fighting broke out. In the confusion, barrels of gunpowder were broken open and almost inevitably there was an explosion in the committee house; 120 people were killed and many nearby buildings damaged. The next day some of the rebels were shot in the castle ditches and the city had to submit to Parliament.

Norfolk did produce one extremist, Miles Corbett of Sprowston, who was the M.P. for Yarmouth. He was a signatory of Charles I's death warrant in 1649 and at the Restoration was hanged at Tyburn as a regicide.

While the nation was in religious and political ferment, there were those who could continue with their everyday life, seemingly unaffected. In 1637 Thomas Browne, a doctor, moved to Norwich, where he lived until his death in 1682. His writings are regarded as some of the finest prose in the English language. His first, and perhaps most famous work, *Religio Medici*, was published in December 1642, a few months after the outbreak of war. It dealt with his religious faith and its relation to his profession. As well as his writings, Browne spent much time in experiments and in the observation of natural phenomena, as well as on his duties as a physician. Throughout his life he remained on equally friendly terms with Royalists such as the Pastons as well as Parliamentarians like the Hobarts.

In 1660 Charles II was restored and the Anglican church re-established. Thomas Browne noted in 1661 that 'Lent was observed this year [for the first time since the Civil War] which made Yarmouth and fishermen rejoice'.

5

Changes in the Countryside

The economic changes which accompanied the establishment of the Tudor dynasty brought both prosperity and hardship to Norfolk. The wet lands of the fens and the Broads were still largely undrained and were used mainly for seasonal grazing. Their inhabitants were engaged in wild-fowling and fishing, while the fertile soils on the periphery produced good crops of cereals and marsh hay. In the heavy clays of mid- and southern Norfolk, areas of forest such as Wayland Wood survived, and cleared land was more suited to pasture than to arable farming. This area was often enclosed at an early date and held by small independent farmers with little need for the co-operative system of farming based on the manor. However, the manor and its lord were still powerful in the 16th century as the manor court had to administer tenancy changes and rent payments, as well as settle land disputes.

73 *Norfolk Horn sheep.*

This farming system contrasted with that found over the light soils and loams of much of the rest of Norfolk, where villages were clustered round the great houses. Here it was sheep rather than cattle that dominated the livestock enterprises, and most of them were owned by landlords rather than working farmers. The area was farmed under a system unique to Norfolk and north-west Suffolk known as 'fold course'. Under this, the manorial lord had the right to graze his sheep over his tenants' strips in the open fields after the harvest until sowing next spring. He also had the right to graze on fallow land in the summer. The manure which the sheep dropped was of great the benefit to the arable crops. The tenant was often allowed to run a few sheep in his lord's flock, and his cattle were allowed on the open fields with the sheep in the winter. This system should have been mutually beneficial, but it led to great social divisions. The landowners became the owners of great flocks with sometimes as many as 15,000 sheep, while the tenants, precluded from owning more than a few sheep and cows, relied on their arable crops for income, which were not as lucrative as sheep.

Below the lesser gentry were the smaller yeomen and tenant farmers, and below them the landless labourers. The day workers were the least secure of this group. They were paid about 6d. a day in the winter and 7d. in the summer in the 1590s, and more for specialised work and at harvest. By 1650 this had risen to between 10d. and a shilling. The yearly hired labourers often lived in the farmhouse; to their 30s. a year, rising

74 *Detail of plaster work in the Long Gallery, Blickling Hall.*

75 *Traditional timber-framed and claylump barn at Forncett St Mary.*

76 *A farm at Bircham Tofts in 1800.*

to 50s. by 1650, must be added the benefit of their board and lodgings. Although wages were rising at about the same rate as the normal price of wheat, the labourers could suffer great deprivation in years of poor harvest. They probably ate very little wheaten bread, mostly rye. The large amount of petty crime reported in the Tudor period suggests that many people were on the verge of pauperism, which was to become an increasing problem in following centuries.

A great variety of crops was grown. Norfolk and Suffolk were the first counties to grow hops; barley was already the most important grain crop and a valuable export, followed by wheat and rye. Oats, peas, vetches and buckwheat were grown for fodder. The area around Walsingham was noted for its saffron. The prosperity of Norfolk farming in the 16th century is shown by the great variety of tools and vehicles listed in inventories; some farms were as large as 300 acres, which would have provided a very comfortable living.

Although landless labourers probably made up a minority of the population in the 16th and 17th centuries, there were many smallholdings. Those less than 10 acres could not have supported a man and his family without some other source of income; between 10 and 60 acres would have provided enough to support a family, but not in affluence.

77 *Interior of a barn from a watercolour by Miles Edmund Cotman (undated, early 19th century).*

The fold-course system, with its benefits for both manorial sheep barons and small arable farmers, only worked when there was complete co-operation between landlord and tenant, but 16th-century court rolls are full of instances of landlords abusing the system. The period in which their sheep were allowed on the fields was being increased; tenants' cattle were being excluded and their sheep prevented from joining the flock. Tenants retaliated by consolidating their holdings in the open fields, exchanging strips with their neighbours, fencing them and then refusing to open them for the landlord's animals. Thus the fold-course system gradually collapsed. Its death-knell came with the introduction of turnips as a field crop from the early 17th century; as an autumn-sown crop, their production precluded the use of the fields for winter grazing.

The only place where there was any concerted effort at land improvement in the Stuart period was in the fens, where in 1630 a group of investors headed by the 4th Duke of Bedford employed the famous Dutch engineer Cornelius Vermuyden to produce a scheme for the drainage of 190,000 acres. This involved the construction of the 'Old' Bedford river into which the old drains ran. It is 70 feet wide and 21 miles long, running in a straight line to the sea. Methwold and Feltwell Fens were drained by the digging of Sam's Cut. In 1651 Vermuyden continued his work by digging the 'New' Bedford river, running parallel to the 'Old' one. The space between the two was flooded in winter, providing rich summer grazing. Alongside this major scheme there were several smaller ones, and as a result large blocks of land passed into the hands of investors, usually men of substance, away from the fenland commoners and waterfowlers.

The population of England rose after 1660 and foreign trade was increasing, yet grain prices fell, which suggests that there was no shortage of supply. Norfolk was particularly well situated to export grain to Holland, and by 1794 was in fact exporting more grain than the rest of England put together. The years of the Napoleonic Wars were a boom period for agriculture. Grain prices were rising faster than the value of livestock, and so there was an incentive to increase grain production. Areas like the Breckland which were really unsuitable for wheat were ploughed up and planted.

One of the best managed estates in the late 18th century was undoubtedly that of the Cokes at Holkham. In addition to a long parliamentary career, Thomas William Coke, later Earl of Leicester, took a great interest in agriculture. In 1776 he began to hold his annual sheep-shearings, which developed into important occasions. Amongst other things, they publicised the introduction of the Southdown sheep, which now began to replace the native Norfolk Horn sheep. From 1790 onwards, farming improvements in Norfolk were dominated by Coke. A monument erected to him in Holkham Park shows some of the things that made him famous. Bas-reliefs represent the sheep-shearings, the granting of a lease

78 *Thomas William Coke, 1754-1842.*

and the creation of an irrigation scheme, while a Devon longhorn bull, a Southdown sheep, a seed drill and a plough are represented on the corners of the base. It is significant that not only Coke but some of the tenants and personal friends who helped to make Holkham famous are also shown on this monument to agricultural progress.

The Raynham estate was also famous for the encouragement it gave to progressive farming. Two generations before Coke, Lord Townshend's agricultural enthusiasm had gained him the nickname 'Turnip Townshend'.

However, contemporaries thought that many of the improvements were pioneered not by the great landowners, but by farmers in the north-east. Here wealthy independently-minded owner-occupiers looked across the North Sea to the new crops being grown in Holland and began to follow suit with very good results. One of the first problems to be tackled was that of maintaining soil fertility. Lack of animal fodder meant that a minimum were kept until spring,

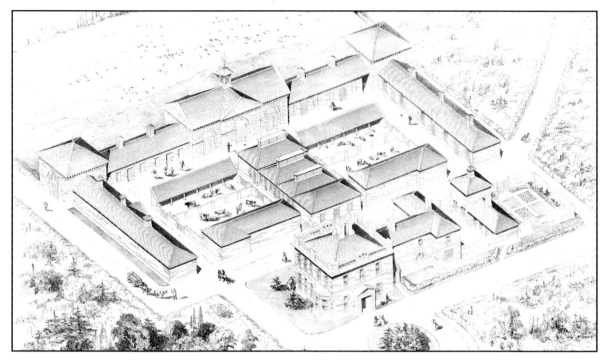

which reduced the quantity of manure available. The only other fertiliser known was the chalky clay called marl. The last option—to leave the land fallow for a year—was not only a waste of land, but in fact put very little good back into the soil. However, from the 16th century new ideas were beginning to circulate. *A Book of Husbandry* (published in 1577) mentioned that rape was cultivated in Cleves as food for sheep, while in the Low Countries turnips and clover were fed to livestock. A winter fodder for livestock enabled more to be kept through the winter, which meant more fresh meat, and more manure. This was particularly valuable if the animals were folded on the turnip fields which they manured as they ate. A root crop, or an 'artificial grass' crop like clover was a much better way of using a fallow year. As early as 1696 a lease for a farm at Waterden stated that the old enclosed fields should not be cropped for more than five years before they were put down to grass. By 1760 turnips and artificial grasses were almost universally grown, but it is not clear how far formal crop rotation was being practised. As a result of these and other improvements in management, rents on the Holkham estate rose by 44 per cent between 1718 and 1759, although there was little rise in agricultural prices.

The change from open field strip farming to enclosed fields was probably the most fundamental change, with social as well as organisational effects. Previously farmers often shared ploughs, horses and manual tasks; now farms were strictly individual units with very small owners often left with unworkably small holdings. It is wrong to think of enclosure as a sudden process, for in many Norfolk parishes it took place

79 *Model Farm, Holkham, built in the 1850s, from a drawing published by the architect, G.A. Dean.*

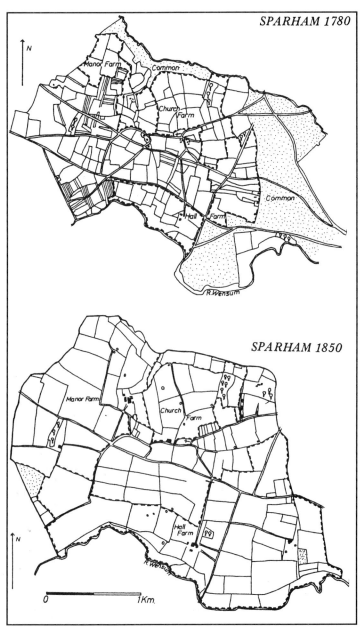

80 *Sparham before and after enclosure.*

over a long period of time, beginning in the 16th century. By 1750, however, there were very few strip fields remaining, and as a result of private exchanges, farms were being consolidated. A 1779 map of Kemp-stone shows considerable areas of strips, but a note explains that the implications were purely legal. Some arrangement to allow a field owned by different owners to be farmed as one could be made, as at Billingford, where a 10½ acre field was held by six owners, yet farmed as a unit.

The 18th and early 19th centuries are traditionally seen as a period of great agricultural improvement, reaching its climax in the 'high farming' of the mid-19th century and followed by agricultural depression and a fall in grain production from the 1870s. Perhaps the part played by Norfolk farmers and their landlords in firstly developing and secondly publicising improved agriculture was the county's most important role in the growth of the national economy.

The 19th-century farming community contained a diverse collection of people. There were the 'gentlemen farmers' for whom farming was not a major source of income. They often concentrated, like the 2nd Earl of Leicester, on breeding pedigree stock. Another group were the wealthy tenant farmers like John Hudson of Castle Acre, who farmed large acreages very intensively and were always ready to try new ideas. Below them were the majority, smaller farmers for whom farming was a way of life, who were often willing to experiment although they lacked capital. The one thing many Norfolk farmers had in common was that their fathers had been there before them. Tenancies were often handed on from father to son. In the small world of landed estates, agents knew each other well and would ask for references for farmers moving from one to another.

The agricultural writer Nathaniel Kent estimated that by 1796 two-thirds of the county was used for arable farming, of which about three-quarters was enclosed, but there was still a considerable amount of common land 'though still a much lesser proportion than in many other counties'. The enclosure of common land was a drastic change which usually took place as a result of a parliamentary Act. Many such enclosures were made during the Napoleonic Wars. The social consequences were serious, as the poor lost their rights to pasture a cow or pig, as well as a fuel supply. These enclosed heaths are usually easily distinguishable: straight roads are flanked by rectangular fields. Often the area of enclosed common is still known as 'the Heath' and is the poorest in the parish, needing much work. The effort involved often seemed too much for farmers, especially in a period of low grain prices, as in the depression following the post-Napoleonic Wars.

The first iron plough was produced in 1770, and by 1808 Robert Ransome, later Ransome, Sims' & Jefferies', firstly of Norwich and then of Ipswich, were making a plough which could easily be dismantled and new parts bolted in. By the middle of the 19th century a number of universal plough bodies were available and by 1896 Ransome's were making 86 different ploughs.

81 *John Hudson, 1824-88, tenant farmer at Castle Acre.*

Early 19th-century farm inventories suggest that a limited range of mechanical equipment was in use. The farm of John Lyall, on the good soils at Dilham near North Walsham, was unusually well equipped in 1836. His machinery included one drawer, one drilling machine, 10 drag rakes, three rolls, two horse carts, one horse drag rake, four pairs of harrows and four ploughs. In the granary was a corn screen, a turnip sowing machine, a scythe and a pair of mangle rollers. There were also forks and rakes as well as a dressing machine.

Although the existence of surplus labour, and the riots that accompanied attempts to introduce threshing machines, discouraged the use of machinery, some were to be found in Norfolk by Arthur Young's visit in 1804. The design of the threshing machine was constantly being improved, and by 1848 Burrell and Sons of Thetford were making a successful one. However, on many farms in the 1840s the crop was still being hand-flailed, especially in the winter when there was little alternative employment. By 1840 a corn and fertilizer drill had been produced that changed little until the introduction of the tractor. By 1850 the method of harvesting the grain crop had changed from reaping with a sickle to mowing with a scythe. The work was still carried out by hand. We have a description of harvest on a farm in Castle Acre in 1843:

Thirty-four men mow the wheat and in order to lay it evenly their scythes are fitted with cradles made of iron rods. These men are each followed by two women ... and a boy or girl to gather up the corn into small sheaves. Eight teamsmen ... follow to shock up the sheaves of which they place ten in a shock ... 300 acres of wheat is cut in six days. Carting takes a further eight. Eighteen to 20 days are needed to complete the harvest.

Although the use of the reaping machine displaced the hand reaper, there was still work for women and children in binding the sheaves and building the stooks, until in the 1870s the mechanical binder was introduced.

The 1840s saw Norfolk farming entering the prosperous mid-century 'golden years'. Four- and six-course crop rotations worked well and cattle feed and fertilisers were produced at home; thus very little needed to be bought in. If the first requirements of a progressive farmer were well laid-out and fertilised fields, secondly he needed a good set of farm buildings in which to store and process his crops, the latter including both the threshing of grain crops and the feeding of fodder to animals. By the late 18th century, buildings were being improved, especially on the Holkham estate. The barns were huge, supposedly because Norfolk farmers liked to keep most of their crop indoors rather than stacking it in a yard. They are a monument to the farmers of the Napoleonic Wars as the wool churches were to the medieval sheep farmers.

82 Aerial view of Crabbs Castle Farm Wighton, showing barn and cattle sheds behind forming the typical E-shape. New buildings have been inserted in the old framework.

Coke of Holkham also redesigned entire farmsteads: between 1790 and 1820 about 30 major rebuilding projects were undertaken on the Holkham estates, 15 of these involving complete rebuildings of farms and premises. One of the earliest was the farm at Waterden. It was visited by the agricultural writer Arthur Young in 1784 who wrote 'Every convenience imagined is thought of, and the offices so perfectly well arranged as to answer the great object, to prevent waste and save labour'.

V   *The 15th-century gate-way at Baconsthorpe Castle.*

VI   *St Benet's Abbey and windmill.*

VII *Burney Arms grinding mill and windpump, with Breydon Water behind. Burney Arms is owned by English Heritage and open to the public.*

83 A marshland farm at Tunstall in the 1930s.

With increasing employment opportunities in the towns, rural under-employment diminished, and there was more incentive to mechanise, although on many small farms hand methods continued to be used well into this century. The increase in machinery led to the building of implement sheds on many farms in the 1860s and 1870s. Often a black-smith's or carpenter's shop was built alongside, so that repairs could be carried out on the premises.

The introduction of chemical fertilisers made it unnecessary to have a year of roots or grass between crops, allowing for even more intensive grain production. As the standard of living of the growing urban population rose, the demand for meat increased, and the prices commanded by fatstock rose. New feeds were introduced, such as linseed and other cattle cake.

Although agriculture was prosperous around 1850, this does not mean that there was complacency amongst farmers. One wrote in 1844 'Production will increase as knowledge itself increases', and this optimism encouraged active research into new methods and the ready acceptance of new ideas. By 1850, 58 per cent of the county's farms were still under 100 acres and 28 per cent were between 200 and 300 acres. Only 1.8 per cent of the county was in farms of over 1,000 acres, and most of these were on the light Breckland soils. Over half the farms under 100 acres were free-hold and it was here that farming was at its worst. The heavy soils of central and southern Norfolk where most of these farms were situated needed draining, and cheap methods of drainage were used because the farmers lacked capital to implement more permanent improvements.

Agriculture was certainly an important employer in Georgian and Victorian Norfolk, but there was a far greater variety of work available in rural areas than there is now. The central Norfolk village of Tittleshall was a large but remote parish. Its population numbered 615 in 1851, when it supported a grocer, a shoemaker, a baker, a draper, and several butchers. There were also bricklayers and makers, thatchers, blacksmiths, wheelwrights, hurdlemakers, and fishermen. Just over half the working population of 215 were agricultural labourers but in only 55 of the 124 dwellings was the head of the family so employed. This pattern was repeated in nearly every mid-19th century Norfolk village, and the variety of employment would have been even greater in the 18th century, when, for instance, village potters supplied local needs and spinning and weaving were still important village industries. The fact that less than half the employed population were full-time agricultural labourers does not mean that the lives of the others were divorced from the land. At harvest time there was work for everyone, and many a craftsman fell back on casual labour in hard times.

Agricultural work itself covered different varieties of employment. The best off were those in charge of livestock. The shepherd, the yardsman who was in charge of the cattle, and the teamsman who looked after the

84 Below. *Women's work—in the field. A member of the women's land army at Thistleton-Smith's farm, West Barsham, 1915.*

85 Below right. *Women's work—at home.*

horses, were always hired for the year and usually provided with a cottage. In the 18th century, labour for most types of farm work was hired annually at hiring fairs, but their importance gradually declined. In 1762 there were at least 25 Norfolk hiring fairs, but by 1822 only three. By the 19th century most labour, except that involved with animals, was hired by the day. There was no pay on wet days, and the labourer was entirely at the mercy of his employer, who could cut wages when prices were low.

Early 18th-century farms were smaller than Victorian ones, and could be run by the farmer and his family with the help of a few 'living-in' servants. As farm sizes increased, farmers needed more labour, and became more distant from their employees. Weekly or daily wages replaced yearly hire and 'living-in'.

86 *Loose boxes for cattle, built at Egmere farm in the 1850s.*

Even for the poorest labourer there were times for recreation and enjoyment. Most could find employment at harvest time, and traditionally the farmer provided a 'frolic' at the end. Occasionally farmers organised an annual outing, particularly with the coming of the railways. When the vicar of Dereham visited Lowestoft in 1856, he met a 'princely and enlightened farmer who had brought 40 of his men to have a day out at the seaside'.

FARM LABOURERS' EARNINGS IN NORFOLK IN 1799 and 1838

A	1799	£	s	d
	48 weeks at 8s. per week	18	4	0
	Harvest—4 weeks	4	14	6
	Wife's earnings 48 weeks at 1s. per week	2	2	0
	Wife's gleanings		14	0
	Total	26	0	6
	Total outgoings	30	9	2

B 1	1838		s	d
	Household weekly accounts based on a wage of 10s. per week			
	2½ stone of flour		6	10½
	Yeast		1	3
	Rent		1	7½
	Coal			10
	Candles			3½
	Total		9	10½

2 Household weekly accounts where more than one member of the family is working

Income			Expenditure	
Man's wages	11s.		Bread	6s. 3d.
Boy (14 years)	5s.		Bacon	1s. 8d.
Boy (11 years)	1s. 6d.		Cheese	1s.
			Butter	1s. 3d.
			Tea and sugar	1s. 9d.
			Flour	5½d.
			Club subscription	9d.
			Tobacco	3d.
			Lights and sundries	9d.
	17s. 6d.			14s. 1½d.

No account of rent has been taken

Wages for the least secure agricultural labourers were very low. Between 1750 and 1800 wages went up by 25 per cent and the cost of living by 60 per cent. Because Norfolk was suffering from overpopulation, labourers were not in a good bargaining position. As late as 1831, an eighth of the men in rural Norfolk were partially or totally unemployed. By the 1790s the worsening conditions had led to enormous increases in the parish poor rates—the amount paid by ratepayers to help the poor within their parish. This encouraged ratepayers to look for an alternative means of poor relief. The answer was the establishment of 'houses of industry'. This involved the grouping together of parishes into 'corporations', for which local legislation was necessary, and then the building of workhouses where the poor had to live and work. An indication of the extreme poverty of Norfolk is the very early date at which workhouses were set up. The earliest rural workhouse was at Heckingham, opened in 1767. By 1834 a third of Norfolk parishes were incorporated and half had access to a workhouse.

At Smallburgh, Rollesby and Gressenhall workhouses, the men were employed on a farm. Women and children undertook spinning for the Norwich manufacturers. In later workhouses families and married couples were separated, but this does not seem to have been the case before 1834. At Smallburgh and Gressenhall there were cottages for elderly married couples.

The conditions of the agricultural labourer reached a very low ebb by 1815, but things got worse. The end of the wars meant that many ex-soldiers were unemployed. Grain prices fell and farmers lowered wages; a landowner-dominated Parliament passed the Corn Laws, which prevented the import of grain until the price of English wheat reached 80 shillings a quarter.

In these circumstances the violent riots that took place in East Anglia in 1816 were not surprising. Rick burning and machine breaking were nothing new. Threshing machines were particularly hated, as they removed a valuable source of winter employment. In April and May 1816 riots broke out around Littleport and Southery in Cambridgeshire, Brandon in Suffolk, and Watton, Downham Market and Norwich in Norfolk, coinciding with a rise in the price of bread and flour. Although the riots were directed against property rather than persons, nine men and six women were sentenced to death, although only two were actually executed. In the autumn of 1830 a new wave of riots affected Norfolk. These were the 'Swing' riots, so-called because a threatening letter signed by 'Captain Swing' often preceded a disturbance. As previously, labourers demanded wage increases and the removal of threshing machines, 29 of which were broken.

Evidence for cottage conditions in 18th-century Norfolk is very difficult to come by. It seems that as small farms within villages were bought up, farm houses were divided to provide accommodation. There is very little evidence for new cottage building, except for the small 'model villages' on estates such as Houghton. Even there, early 19th-century illustrations of

87 *Inscription on the gable of a barn at Ludham.*

88 *Aerial view of Mitford and Launditch House of Industry (1779), later the Union workhouse and now the headquarters of the county's rural life museum and archaeology service.*

89 *Infants' yard, Mitford and Launditch Union Workhouse, 1935-6.*

90 *A 19th-century cottage interior.*

cottages away from the 'model village' show many were very dilapidated, held up with wooden shoring and with decayed sagging roofs. The building materials available were not very good. Brick and flint with a pantile roof was best, but most cottages, especially in the south of the county, were built of clay lump, with thatched roofs.

By the 1840s the majority of people had a two-roomed house, perhaps with a 'back-house' or scullery added on. Much was written about the improvement of cottages, yet very little was done. Articles in the *Norfolk News* published between 1863 and 1864 described the poor conditions:

> We have recently seen a farm where thousands have been expended on magnificent stalls and outbuildings for horses and cattle, and within a few hundred yards stand miserable huts, through the roofs of which the stars may be seen at night.

Although the population continued to increase, accommodation did not. Much of the blame for this can be put upon the 17th-century settlement laws, which made the ratepayers of each parish responsible for those born or claiming a settlement within that parish. This was clearly an incentive for the ratepayers to discourage settlement; so new houses were not built and old ones left to fall down. Several cottages in Flitcham housed seven inhabitants but had only one bedroom. A cottage at Wighton, surprisingly described as 'clean and neat', had one bedroom and ten inhabitants.

If the extra labour needed could not live in estate cottages, it had to travel from elsewhere. It was from this need that the 'gang system' developed. In villages not controlled by one landlord, rows of very poor cottages were erected by speculators, who charged high rents because of the housing shortage. Castle Acre, where in 1851 nine people were described as 'owners of houses', was one such 'open village'. Labourers would travel from these villages to work, often over many miles, and were organised by 'gang masters' into gangs which were hired out to farms to do specific tasks, such as turnip hoeing, weeding or digging up potatoes.

Underemployment continued to be a problem as the population steadily rose, which meant that poor rates continued to rise. This led to agitation amongst ratepayers nationally for a reform of the Poor Law to bring it under central control, and to abolish all relief to the poor outside workhouses. As a result, the 1834 Poor Law Amendment Act was passed, and in Norfolk 18 new Poor Law Unions and 12 new workhouses were established. The 'paupers' were divided into categories by age, sex and state of health and each category was housed separately. All the different groups had to be under the watchful eye of the master, which led to the spoke-like layout of many workhouses, such as that at Thursford, where the central hub was occupied by the master and the different spokes housed different categories. Work was to be of the most tedious and repetitive type, less pleasant than work outside. Unmarried mothers were always treated almost as criminals. An instruction went out at Swaffham in 1838 that they 'should be put in a dress of different colour from other women; that boards should be made and put up against the windows in [their] sleeping room'. However, people in the workhouse could be sure of regular if monotonous meals, and of some sort of education for their children, which they were unlikely to receive outside.

The 1834 Act had made very little provision for the sick, yet this became one of the greatest problems for the Poor Law Guardians. The mentally sick were largely ignored, and 'harmless idiots' lived with other inmates. Poor Law medical officers were appointed, who were generally better qualified than the village quacks usually consulted by the poor. By 1896, 145 nurses were employed in Norfolk workhouses.

Many Unions sponsored emigration schemes. Between 1835 and 1837, 3,354 people from Norfolk villages went to Canada. Others were helped to move to the industrial north. It was, however, the able and ambitious who left, leaving the older and less capable behind.

The introduction of the new Poor Law was very much resented by the poor. There were riots at Rollesby and a wall with gun slits was erected around the site of Pulham Market workhouse, manned by the local militia, to prevent it being pulled down whilst it was being erected.

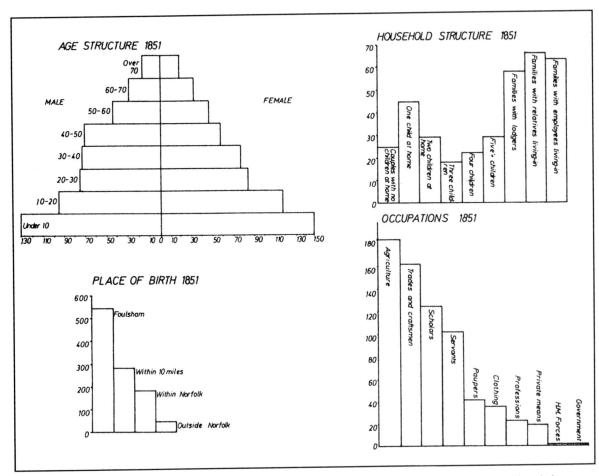

91 *Foulsham 1851,*
from the census statistics.

Between 1851 and 1861 the population actually declined by two per cent. This, together with the fact that agriculture was entering the prosperous years of the mid-century, helped to improve the conditions of the poor and to bring down the poor rate. As general conditions improved, the attitudes of the Poor Law Guardians relaxed and became more humane. After 1865, the Union Chargeability Act provided that there should be a flat poor rate throughout the Union and not a different one for each parish. It was no longer beneficial to keep down the population within the individual parishes, and farmers now argued that a workforce living near its work would be more reliable. During the 1860s and 1870s many cottages were built, usually substantial brick and pantile houses. By 1887 a third of the Blickling estate cottages had three bedrooms. Most were described as 'clean and comfortable', only one as 'overcrowded'. By the end of the century cottage conditions had much improved.

The years of high prices and agricultural boom lasted until the 1870s, and the area of land cropped steadily increased throughout this period. There were 1,005,135 acres in Norfolk under crop in 1854 and 1,086,767 in 1882. The amount of wheat declined, while barley increased. In spite of sporadic outbreaks of foot and mouth disease, the number of cattle and pigs increased between 1854 and 1882, but the number of sheep declined.

In the 1870s, grain prices fell. The price on Norwich market fell from 65s. a quarter in 1872 to below 55s. the following year. Contemporaries blamed the fall on bad harvests and rising wages. With the decline in rural population, higher industrial wages, and attempts amongst labourers to unionise, wages rose from an average of nine to 10 shillings a week, to 13 or 14 shillings. In the 1840s rents had been twice the labour bill; by the 1880s, it was the other way round.

92 *Workhouse doll in the uniform of a child.*

However, the real cause of the depression was foreign competition. Grain from North America was finding its way on to the British market, and from 1891 stock farmers also suffered when refrigerated ships began to bring meat from the New World. Wool prices had already fallen as a result of Australian and New Zealand imports. High grade malting barley, however, could still command a good price, and so farmers turned to more mixed farming systems. Attempts were also made to find less labour-intensive methods. Farmers in fertile areas suffered least, those on the heavy clay lands most severely.

The long-established family dynasties of farming tenants began to disappear in the depression, and landlords could no longer be particular about whom they took on. Advertisements were placed in Scottish newspapers, and many Scots took over East Anglian farms. The new men often brought capital made outside agriculture and with it were able to restock their farms and also introduce more mechanisation, whilst maintaining their non-farming interests. Rents dropped by as much as a half, and newcomers often asked for improvements and additions to be made to the buildings before agreeing to come. The author and Norfolk landlord Rider Haggard wrote that 'the old stamp of tenant farmer is ceasing to exist. In his place has arisen a new style of person, who, unless the land be in tip-top condition when he may venture on a four-year lease, will only farm from year to year'.

By the end of the century it was clear that livestock prices were keeping up better than those of grain, and a less intensive form of management, laying down semi-permanent pasture, was often practised. The acreage of permanent pasture in Norfolk increased by nearly a third between 1870 and 1890. Another indication of the decline in intensive farming is in the reduction in the number of horses kept: declining by 10,000 from an 1871 total of 56,000 over 20 years. The only type of agriculture to expand significantly was horticulture.

Although change was slow, the face of the county was very different in 1914 from that of 100 years previously. The open common land had nearly all gone. Farms were better laid out, and had groups of substantial farm buildings. There were fewer farm labourers, and fewer wealthy farmers. Most small farmers, however, probably continued to farm in much the same way with the help of their families.

93 *Workhouse doll in the uniform of an old lady.*

94 *George Edwards.*

The second half of the 19th century saw the increasing importance of trade unions in many industries, but the organisation of unions in the country was far more difficult. Up to the 1830s riots rather than strikes had been the farm labourer's weapon. Workers who lived in tied cottages and who had little prospect of alternative local employment were unlikely to strike. When George Edwards became a union secretary in Norfolk, he was continually being forced to move until he found employment outside farming in the more casual set-up of a brick kiln.

By the 1860s, however, things were beginning to change. Labour was scarcer, and the men were beginning to become interested in unions. One farmer complained that 'you will see teamsters sitting on their corn bins, reading their penny newspapers, when at the same time they should be grooming and feeding their masters' horses'. Many learnt the art of public speaking at Primitive Methodist chapels, and chapel buildings were frequently made available for union meetings.

From 1865 onwards harvests were poor, and by 1868 farmers had begun reducing wages. Village unions mushroomed throughout Norfolk in the spring of 1872—isolated groups, often with different aims, some emphasising the religious and others the economic side of the movement. Their leaders were not all labourers, but came from the higher ranks of working men. Mr. Applegate of Aylsham was the foreman of Blickling brickyard, and Mr. Rix of Swanton Morley was a shopkeeper. By the summer there were unions in Thetford, Swaffham, Fakenham, East Dereham, Attleborough, Blofield, North Walsham and Aylsham.

The formation of unions increased the rift between farmers and workers. The Farmers' Defence Association was formed in 1873, but was not supported by all landlords; Lords Leicester and Suffield refused to join any combination of employer against employed.

The Norwich press took an interest in the new trade unions, and reported most of their activities sympathetically. Several strikes were called and these were often followed by lock-outs, which themselves encouraged emigration to the towns. There were attempts at solidarity with urban workers, but these failed because townsmen were often prepared to act as blackleg labour. As the agricultural depression deepened, the unions found it impossible to resist wage reductions, and by the end of 1878 both the Lincolnshire Labourers' League and the National Agricultural Labourers' Union had fizzled out in Norfolk.

Unionism revived between 1890-6, but it was not until 1906, when George Edwards became secretary of the Eastern Counties Agricultural Labourers' Union, that it was established permanently. By 1908 it had 5,000 members and was affiliated to the T.U.C. Edwards, who had begun work as a boy scaring crows, eventually became a Labour M.P. He was able to speak for the agricultural labourers whose living conditions were still far below those of other workers. The voice of farm workers had changed from that of a rick-burning rabble to a parliamentary force.

6

The Gentry

Pre-industrial society was dominated by class. Position was governed by birth, education and, most important of all, the ownership of land. Even in Victorian England, land gave status, but with the breakdown of feudal society it became possible for the *nouveaux riches* to buy into landed society. The Tudor and early Stuart period was one of high inflation. Prices rose three-fold from 1570 to 1640, but income from sheep farming more than made up for this. The owner of about 1,000 sheep in 1540 could hope to make about £40 per annum profit, whilst 100 years later he would make about £140. It is not surprising, then, that enormous fortunes were made from sheep farming. The Fermour family, who built the impressive brick manor house of East Barsham Hall, kept sheep on 25 different fold-courses in the 1520s, and owned about 17,000 animals in all. The Heydons of Baconsthorpe entertained 30 shepherds to Christmas dinner in the 1570s and there were several more Norfolk families with between 10,000 and 20,000 sheep.

Below the great sheep magnates were a large number of smaller gentry, gradually building up their estates. For them, sheep farming was not a quick way to wealth, but a dependable livelihood and, if they rented out land as well, they could be sure of a rising income. Their wealth is shown by the large number of manor houses built in this period. Changing lifestyles meant a greater desire for privacy than was possible in the old medieval halls. Many of these 16th- and 17th-century manor houses are still standing, though many have been much altered. The high quality of the workmanship is apparent: the ornate porches are particularly striking, often with more than one storey. Blickling, built between 1619 and 1627 for Sir Henry Hobart, and the earlier example of East Barsham, are only the finest of a very large group of substantial brick and half-timbered houses built in this period.

The buying of an estate was obviously the best form of investment available, and the dissolution of the monasteries provided a ready supply of land in the early 16th century. The aristocracy did not buy much Norfolk monastic land, although the Duke of Norfolk purchased some. Instead, most of the county's 227 monastic manors found their way into the hands of the lesser gentry. Nicholas Bacon, the son of a sheep reeve at the Abbey of St Edmundsbury, rose through the legal profession to become Attorney in the Court of Augmentations, which in the 1530s was responsible for the

95 *Oxburgh Hall, brick gatehouse.*

75

96 *The Tudor manor house of East Barsham Hall.*

selling of monastic lands. He bought lands on his own account in Essex, Hertfordshire and Norfolk. Bacon's major Norfolk purchase was at Stiffkey; altogether he spent just over £7,000 in the county.

A second newcomer to Norfolk landowning society was another lawyer, Edward Coke. He too rose through a career in the law, and became Attorney General in 1593. His purchases laid the foundations of the great 40,000-acre Coke estates; by 1634 he had spent £10,000 on monastic lands.

The 18th century saw a further influx of 'new men' into the ranks of the Norfolk gentry, but, as Norfolk was far from the centres of industry, very few *nouveaux riches* came here. Instead, it was local men who had made their money outside agriculture who looked for Norfolk estates. By the 1870s the Gurneys, an 18th-century banking family, owned at least 5,000 acres and the Lacons, who had been brewers in Yarmouth, owned over a thousand. John Ketton, who had made his fortune selling animal feeds, bought Felbrigg Hall in 1863. Over half the county was farmed in estates of over 1,000 acres in 1870, and 19 per cent of these were over 10,000 acres, yet large landowners never came to dominate Norfolk, as they did in some other areas.

The centre of any estate was the owner's house, which varied widely in size and grandeur. Raynham Hall, the home of the Townshends, was built of red brick in 1622: the architectural historian Nikolaus Pevsner describes it as the 'paramount house' of its date in Norfolk. Mannington Hall, an imposing moated manor, dates from the 15th century, although it was much altered and gothicised by the Earl of Orford in the 19th century. The Astley home at Melton Constable is a fine example of a late Stuart house. The 18th century saw the building of Kimberley (1712) and of Gunton, built in 1741 for Lord Suffield by Matthew Brettingham, as well as the erection of an imposing Palladian mansion at Holkham for the Coke family. Interest in building continued into the 19th century, when many earlier houses were drastically altered and new ones built. The Rev. Henry Lombe commissioned Sir Charles Barry to build Bylaugh

97 *Aerial view of Holkham Hall within its Victorian formal gardens.*

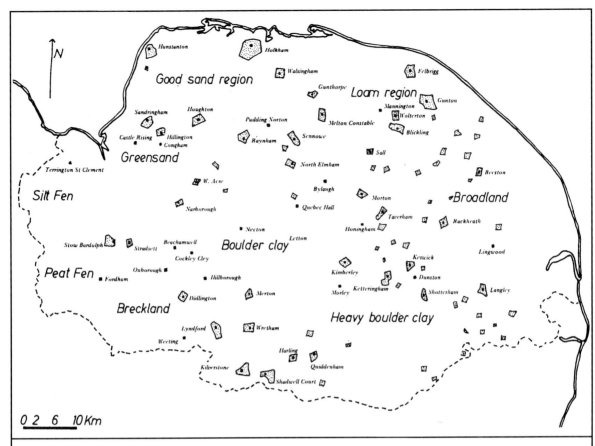

Only the houses of families owning more than 1,000 acres in 1872 are shown. The parks marked are those on Faden's map of Norfolk (1803 edition). Where the park was no longer the centre of an estate in 1872 no house is marked in it.

The main period of construction of the country seats shown on the map

Medieval	Castle Rising		Letton
	Mannington (much restored in		Pudding Norton
	19th century)		Quidenham
			Salle
Tudor	Hunstanton (much 19th-century work)		Shotwell Court
	Terrington St Clements		Shotesham
	Narborough (much 19th-century work)		Walsingham
	Stradsett		West Acre
	Fordham		Wolterton
	Oxborough		
	Norton (much 19th-century work)	19th century	Cockley Clecy
	Morley		Congham
			Dunston
Jacobean	Blickling		Hillington
	Felbrigg		Keswick
	Honingham		Lynford
	Kilverstone (much 19th-century work)		Quebec Hall
	Melton Constable		Rackheath
	Raynham		Sandringham
			Sennow
18th century	Beeston		Stow Bardolph
	Gunthorpe (much 19th-century work)		Taverham
	Gunton	Demolished	Beachamwell
	Hillborough	or rebuilt	Bylaugh
	Holkham	since 1914	Merton
	Houghton		North Elmham
	Kimberley		Weeting
	Langley		Wretham

98 *Family seats in Norfolk.*

Hall (now a ruin) in mock Tudor style. The grandest new house, however, was undoubtedly Sandringham, a Jacobean-style house begun in
1870. Some charming smaller houses also remain on smaller estates, at
Langley, Letton and Shotesham, for instance. This interest in building
and architectural alteration reflects the general prosperity of the gentry,
and the stability of their position until the end of the Victorian era.

99 *The temple,*
Holkham Park.

Only about 10 deer parks were marked on Morden's early 18th-
century map of Norfolk, but the importance of wooded or semi-wooded
parkland increased as the popularity of shooting parties grew, and by
1810 there were nearly 100 scattered over much of the county. During
the 19th century the sport continued to be ever more fashionable, reaching
its height on the Sandringham estate where 28,000 birds a season were
regularly bagged by the 1890s. Although Coke of Holkham had declared
that 'a good understanding between landlord and tenantry' was essential
to estate management, shooting was one area where the interests of the
two groups were at cross purposes. It was always very much resented by
farmers because of the damage game did to crops, as was hunting, another
popular aristocratic sport. However, by the late 19th century, sport was
sometimes considered more valuable than agriculture, particularly on the
poor breckland soils. Estates were sold purely for their game to owners
who took no interest in local affairs. The problems of holiday homes and
absentee owners are not new to Norfolk.

Hospitality played an important part in country house life. The largest
house parties were held in the shooting season, but after the arrival of
the railways, weekend parties became fashionable. We may well wonder
how the Georgian and Victorian upper classes managed to eat so much.
Parson Woodforde of Weston Longville in the late 18th century certainly
dined well. The supper which he ate with the squire at Weston Hall in
June 1783 was typical: 'We had for dinner some beans and bacon, a
chine of mutton roasted, giblet pie, hashed goose, a rabbit roasted and
some young peas—tarts, puddings and jellies'.

Although a picture of warm hospitality and comfort is the usual
image of the country house, a description of life at Hunstanton Hall in
the 1850s, as remembered by a member of the Le Strange family, will
correct the balance. The life of these children was frugal. There were no
carpets and little furniture in their quarters. Few candles were allowed,
because of the very real risk of fire. Their food was simple and their
education rigorous.

His house and his park, his sport and his entertaining, must have
taken up much of the landowner's time, but he had far-reaching
responsibilities towards the nation and his local community. The country
gentry had always played an essential part in the maintenance of law
and order, mainly through their work as Justices of the Peace. During
the 18th century, their duties increased to include the prevention of riots,
the supervision of alehouses, the condition of roads and bridges, the
regulation of markets and the enforcement of the Poor Law. In the
following century, however, many of these responsibilities were taken

100 *Preparing lunch for a shooting party, Bylaugh Park, c.1907.*

101 *Aerial photograph of Houghton Hall.*

VIII *Castle Rising Castle, owned by English Heritage and open to the public.*

IX *Estate workshops in Holkham park, built in the 1850s to service the 40,000-acre estate. The clock tower is above the clerk of works' office.*

X *The Great Barn at Holkham, built in the 1790s as the back cloth to the famous Holkham sheep shearings.*

from them. After 1834, for instance, the care of the poor was in the hands of the Poor Law Guardians. County councils were introduced in 1888, leaving J.P.s with little except their legal duties.

Landowners were much sought after as presidents of local charitable and academic societies. Many took an interest in history and antiquarian studies, and were members of the Council of the Norfolk and Norwich Archaeological Society. They collected works of art and fine libraries, many of which can be seen in those stately homes which have been opened to the public. The gentry and nobility provided a focus of local interest which is hard to understand today: the whole village would hold celebrations at family births and weddings, and funerals always produced demonstrations of public sympathy. The most memorable 19th-century funeral must have been that of Coke of Holkham in 1842. 'The procession was two miles long when it started, but at every crossroad along the route numbers were waiting to join it ... when the hearse finally drew up at the door of the church, the line of carriages alone reached to Litcham, two and a half miles away'.

102 *Sir Robert Walpole.*

Candidates for parliamentary seats were drawn from a very small group. They needed huge fortunes, for not only were they expected to entertain their supporters, and possibly even to bribe them, but they also had to transport them to the poll. They also needed 'standing', which really meant that they came from old county families. All the six families who provided M.P.s for the county between 1750 and 1820 could boast uninterrupted residence and continued importance within Norfolk for 400 years. The 18th century saw several Norfolk politicians rise to high office. The Walpoles had been a long-established county family for many generations before Robert Walpole became George I's chief minister, and Charles Townshend, Walpole's fellow Secretary of State, was from a family which had owned the land round Raynham for centuries. William Windham of Felbrigg was a M.P. from 1784 to 1810 and Secretary for War from 1794 to 1801.

103 *Rider Haggard in his garden at Ditchingham.*

The county sent two members to Parliament, whilst Norwich, Yarmouth, King's Lynn, Thetford and Castle Rising each sent two more. Elections were firmly controlled by the Earl of Suffolk and the Walpoles at Castle Rising, and the Duke of Grafton and Lord Petre at Thetford. In the county, the electorate consisted of about 5,000 40 shilling freeholders (an eighth of the county's adult males) at the beginning of the 19th century. In Norwich, the number of voting freemen rose from 2,300 in 1761 to 4,000 in 1831; in Yarmouth from 700 to 1,700. In Lynn there were consistently about 300 voters. Gentry influence over the 40 shilling freeholders took various forms. Tenants were expected to follow their landlord's guidance in voting, and clergymen, the wishes of their patrons. Others responded to business put their way, and other

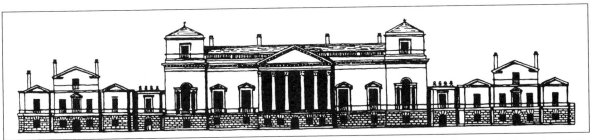

104 *Holkham Hall, south front.*

105 *The game larder, Holkham Hall.*

kindnesses shown. The introduction of electoral reforms during the 19th century gradually reduced the power of the gentry over voters, by such innovations as the secret ballot, and by the expansion of the electorate to a size where no private individual's means would suffice to buy him votes.

By the end of the Victorian era the position of the gentry was very different from that it had enjoyed when George I came to the throne. They were no longer the wealthiest group in society: many industrialists could boast of larger fortunes. With declining agricultural prosperity and falling rents the ownership of land was no longer so profitable, although ownership of it still gave prestige. Their parliamentary influence was greatly lessened, although probably still greater in rural Norfolk than elsewhere. The gentry's lifestyle had also changed. As travel became easier, many were away from home much of the time: as rents declined, many chose to live in simpler style in spas and resorts in England or abroad, like the Rolfe family from Heacham who joined other voluntary English exiles in Naples.

Smaller landlords were forced to take a more personal interest in the management of their estates, as tenants could no longer be found so easily. In earlier years, agents maintained close control over tenants, and felt entitled to write letters like this one from the Blickling agent to a Mr. Ladell: 'I was surprised to observe how small a proportion of your farm is in turnips. This ought not to be and cannot be allowed'. This lordly domination of tenants' farm management, as of their electoral freedoms, was no longer possible by the end of the 19th century.

106 *Sandringham House, east front.*

107 *Raynham Hall.*

7

Towns, Trade and Industry

The growing prosperity of the Tudor countryside was reflected in the towns. The population of Norwich at this time was about 10,000, and in the taxation of 1523-7 the city contributed £1,704, more than any other provincial city. By Elizabeth's reign the basis of its wealth had broadened. Weaving was still important, but the city had also become the centre for an increasingly wealthy local gentry. Between 1525 and 1569 the number of freemen engaged in the distribution and clothing trades (such as grocers, haberdashers, tailors and cordwainers) nearly quadrupled, while the number of those employed in textiles remained static. The grocers were the richest and most influential group; nearly half the Elizabethan mayors were drawn from their ranks.

However, problems in the economy were apparent. Exports of worsted had declined, and this affected other industries: craftsmen from the building trade as well as weavers were leaving the city. In 1524 a desperate attempt was made to restore Norwich's position: the government ordered that all worsted cloth, wherever it was woven, should be finished there, but this had little effect and the city continued to decline.

Given the depression in the worsted trade and the agricultural unrest in the countryside, it is not surprising that there were several rebellions in the first half of the 16th century. The early ones were concerned with the enclosure of land for sheep walks, but the causes of 'Kett's Rebellion' in 1549 were more serious, and led to a major conflict at Norwich. The episode began in Wymondham. The priory church had been shared between the monks and the parishioners and there had long been disputes over responsibility for upkeep. After the Reformation the monastery was scheduled for demolition under the supervision of the local Crown Agent, Sir John Flowerdew. The parishioners feared this would damage their part of the church and asked the king's permission to buy the portions of the monastery which were structurally part of the church. It was granted, but Flowerdew continued demolition.

On 8 July, a large crowd gathered for the festival of St Thomas; it became disorderly and set off to pull down Flowerdew's fences. He met them, bribed them to go away and suggested they pull down those of

108 *A group of 16th-century pots from Fulmodeston.*

109 *Morley Old Hall, c.1580.*

Robert Kett, a small landowner who had enclosed land. When the mob arrived Kett joined them as their leader; the reasons for his action are unknown. The next day he led the crowd to Norwich, where they camped outside the walls from 12 July to 27 August, and drew up a list of 29 grievances. Mostly these demands concerned the right of the common man to use land, to be charged reasonable rents and to a fair unbiased hearing in cases involving the laws of real property. They were not directly concerned with religion, but they did want to see clerical wealth limited and parochial duties properly performed. These rebels were not landless labourers, but small farmers and tradesmen.

However, the government was not prepared to see Kett as an ally against local corruption; it ordered the rebels to disperse and Norwich to stand firm against them. Kett would not obey, and took control of the city. Although the Earl of Northampton, who had been sent to put down the rebellion, entered Norwich, his forces could not hold it and were forced to retreat. After his failure, the Earl of Warwick was sent with a new army and took Norwich. Without the city, Kett had no source of supplies and was forced into battle at a site probably in the parishes of either Sprowston or Thorpe, called 'Dussingdale'. Warwick won, and perhaps 3,000 men died. On 28 August executions began. Kett and his brother were tried in London but brought back to Norfolk for execution, Robert at Norwich Castle and his brother at Wymondham. After this, Norfolk was peaceful for the rest of the Tudor period.

After 1554 Norwich's prosperity began to improve slowly with the arrival of refugee Dutch weavers. By 1579 about 6,000 'strangers' out of a total population of 16,000 had settled in Norwich. As well as the Dutch there was a small group of French-speaking Protestants (Walloons). These groups were largely responsible for the restoration of Norwich to its position as a major weaving centre.

Even with this upturn in her economy, Norwich could not escape the problems of poverty amongst her poorest inhabitants. The Mayor complained that about one-fifth of the population were living on charity. Between 1570 and 1580 beggars were banned. Those giving to them were fined, and tramps were arrested and whipped. However, Norwich was the first city to adopt a regular system of poor relief (by 1570) which included not only financial help, but also education for pauper children. An outbreak of plague in 1579 added to the city's problems, and there was little population increase until after the end of the century.

After 1600 Norwich weavers themselves began to make 'Dutch cloths' and to sell them under the name of 'Norwich stuffs'. Norfolk wool was not suitable, and wool of the right staple had to be imported from else-where. The early 17th century saw a population expansion to about 32,000 by 1622. In 1600, the diarist John Harrington described Norwich as 'another Utopia, the people live so orderly, the streets kept so cleanly, the tradesmen, young and old, so industrious, the better sort so provident and withall so charitable that it is as rare to meet a beggar there as it is common at Westminster'. Perhaps the earlier statutes against begging had proved effective! The high level of literacy amongst the citizens is shown by the fact that the first provincial lending library was started here in 1608.

By 1700 Norwich was the largest provincial city, although by 1730 it had been overtaken by Bristol. Perhaps as much as half the population were engaged in cloth production. Yarn was mostly spun in the country-side, but increasingly weaving was concentrated in Norwich. The

110 *Norwich Yarn Company, 1839.*

dominance of the industry is illustrated in Daniel Defoe's account of his visit in 1722:

> If a stranger were to ride through or view the city of Norwich for a day, he would have reason to think that here was a town without inhabitants; but on the contrary, if he was to view the city, either on a Sabbath day or any public occasion, he would wonder where all the people could dwell, the multitude is so great. But the case is this: the inhabitants being all busy at their manufacture dwell in their combing-shops, twisting-mills and other work houses.

Most of these concerns were small businesses carried on in the city's upper garrets. A master craftsman would work with a few journeymen and apprentices. The majority of the population were poor but not penniless, independently-minded artisans. However, a small group of very wealthy clothiers and merchants controlled the city's life.

The nature of the cloth trade was changing, and instead of much of it going for export, most was now sold in England, being suited to the semi-fashionable market amongst the middle classes. The city attempted to limit competition, especially from imported Indian cotton. In 1721 a parliamentary Act prohibited the general wearing of cotton.

111 *Thomas Paine, 1737-1809.*

Despite the importance of the cloth trade, Norwich's real strength lay in its broadly-based economy, with other industries such as tanning and leatherworking, malting and brewing. There were also skilled craftsmen like silversmiths working there. The city was a fashionable centre with a theatre and assembly rooms by 1750, and its own newspaper from 1727.

The 18th century saw a growing threat to the hand-weavers from the increasing use of mechanisation in the north of England. Norwich manufacturers tried to counter this by concentrating on high-quality goods which could not be machine-made. From the 1790s cloths of a mixture of worsted and silk, or worsted and cotton were produced. They were often highly coloured, as Norwich dyeing had always been of a high standard. Efforts were made to imitate the fashionable, but expensive, imported Indian shawls. By 1802 there were 12 shawl-making establishments in Norwich, and many of their products were exported to America. Looms were developed that wove in the outline of a pattern, leaving the flowers to be hand-embroidered, and eventually others appeared which wove the entire pattern in.

Norwich cloth was light, well-finished and attractive. It was also cheap as wages were 40 per cent lower than those in the rival city of Exeter. Nevertheless, machine-made Lancashire cottons began to capture the English market, and Norwich had to rely increasingly upon her exports, which meant that she was badly affected by the breakdown of European trade during the Napoleonic Wars. During the 1790s the population actually fell, and in 1801 8½ per cent of the housing stock was uninhabited.

A combination of unaccustomed poverty and the independent nature traditionally associated with the Norwich handloom weavers led to the development of a strong revolutionary movement in the city. The Prime Minister, William Pitt, described it as the 'Jacobin city'. There were many radical clubs supporting the French and denouncing the war, and numerous outspoken pamphlets circulated.

Norwich was not only an active city politically, but also in the realm of ideas. Andrew Robertson, a distinguished miniaturist and friend of Constable, visited the city in 1812. He wrote:

> I arrived here a week ago and find it a place where the arts are very much cultivated ... some branches of knowledge, chemistry, botany, etc., are carried to a great length. General literature seems to be pursued with an ardour which is astonishing when we consider that it does not contain a university and is merely a manufacturing town.

112 *John Sell Cotman, 1782-1824.*

He went on to describe the high quality of the music in the city, and most important, perhaps, the painting and drawing, particularly the water-colour work being executed in and around the city. 'The studies of landscape about the town are infinitely beautiful and inexhaustable. The buildings, cottages etc., are charming'. Several late 18th-century writers and thinkers made their homes here, including Amelia Opie, wife of the portrait painter, a novelist and radical, and the energetic polymath Thomas Dawson. Dawson was not only a patron of artists, but also wrote on many topics, such as art, architecture, botany and travel, whilst running his family bank. Norwich had a large number of artists, who taught and dealt in pictures as well as painting themselves, and who founded the Norwich Society of Artists in 1803. They held meetings and exhibitions, the latter annually from 1805 to 1833. One of the most well-known of their number was the landscape painter John Sell Cotman. Although the 'Norwich School' can be regarded as continuing until the 1880s, its most vital phase ended in 1833.

The tranquillity and timelessness of the scenes these artists produced give only slight hints—for instance, where a dilapidated building is the subject—that Norwich was suffering from an industrial depression and that the slow decline of the handloom weavers in the face of increasing mechanisation had begun. Their wages were barely above starvation levels in the early 19th century, and in 1838 they struck against a further reduction.

In 1839 a textile mill was built beside the river by the Norwich Yarn Company. Steam power was provided, and each floor was let to a different firm. The scale of operation could be far larger than on a domestic basis, and the mill, with its 65 spinning frames and 500 powered looms, remained in operation until it was taken over by Jarrolds, the printers, in 1902.

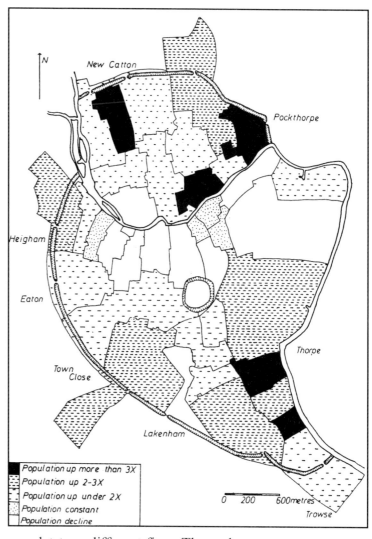

113 *Population changes within Norwich, 1801-1881.*

The importance of Norwich Market increased throughout the 18th century as farmers became more prosperous and had more to sell. A larger cattle market was created by levelling the outer earthworks of the castle and filling in the ditches. Agricultural wealth led to the establishment of banks; there were six in Norwich by 1800. Various insurance companies were established, one of which, the Norwich Union (founded 1797) was to rise to international importance. As an episcopal seat and the home of the law courts, the printing and papermaking industries were encouraged to develop in Norwich. By the 19th century these had become major concerns with Jarrold and Sons setting up printing presses in London Street in 1823

114   *Norwich market place in the early 19th century by J.S. Cotman.*

115   *Norwich livestock market,* c.1900.

and paper mills at Bawburgh and Taverham. Between 1791 and 1801 all the city gates were taken down as obstructions to traffic, and the walls were no longer maintained as the city began to expand outside them. Port activities remained important. Ships taking textiles to India and China returned with luxury goods which found a ready market amongst wealthy Norwich merchants and gentlemen farmers.

Leather working, always important in Norwich, was soon to take over first place as the major employer from the ailing textile industry. Another traditional industry which expanded greatly during the 18th century was brewing. By the early 19th century, brewing in Norwich was dominated by a few large firms. By 1801 John Patteson's brewery was producing 20,000 barrels a year, and by 1836 there were 24 breweries in the city, including several which were to remain important names until after the Second World War.

From being an industrial town principally concerned with the processing of the major raw material of pre-industrial England (wool), Norwich had become the provincial capital of a rich cereal-growing area, well away from the major new centres of industrial development. This meant that although the population almost doubled between 1801 and 1851, Norwich dropped from being the largest provincial town in 1700 to being only the 15th largest by 1850.

Yarmouth and Lynn both increased their prosperity in Elizabethan times with growing exports of grain and imports of coal, which were transported inland along the river systems. Norfolk ports provided a greater tonnage of shipping than any other maritime county. Trade with the Low Countries flourished, but Lynn in particular gained over the Dutch during the war against Spain. The number of Lynn-owned ships registered in the port books rose from 17 to 60 between 1567 and 1587, while the tonnage went up even more.

116 *A Yarmouth Row.*

Lynn was not an industrial town; instead it contained craftsmen who catered for the town and its immediate hinterland. As most of these were small-scale enterprises, there are few records of them. The town fields were let for a wide variety of purposes, including cloth drying, rope making and drying fish. There was a fulling mill on the banks of the Gaywood river: corn milling was the monopoly of the Corporation, who had a mill astride the Millfleet. The importance of brewing is shown by the special water pipe, known as 'the brewers' pipe' which ran down King Street. Wealthy merchants enlarged and improved their houses; towers, like that at Clifton House, gave grandeur to existing buildings.

After the establishment of a new town council by the Charter of Incorporation in 1524 great efforts were made to improve the town. Lynn was in advance of many other towns in having a public water supply by the end of the 16th century. Between 1500 and 1700 nearly all the warehouses along the river had been replaced by more spacious buildings. Despite outbreaks of plague in 1587 and 1636, the town prospered; by the end of the 17th century, Defoe described it as 'a beautiful, well built and well situated town'.

117 *Customs House, King's Lynn, 1683.*

Its position gave it links with a greater system of inland navigation than any other port in England except London. Through this network Lynn was the sole supplier of imports to six counties, of which wine and coal were especially important. Lynn imported more coal than any other port between Newcastle and London. The port continued to flourish in the 18th century although the harbour was silting up. In 1724 it was recommended that the lower section of the Ouse should be canalised. Between 1798 and 1828 a new drain, the Eau Bank Cut, was dug to take the waters of the Ouse to the Wash. It joins the original course of the river about a mile upstream of the Customs House. The effect was to accentuate the movement of water to the west at the mouth of the river, and to speed up the formation of a gravel bank on the east. This meant that boats could no longer dock alongside the warehouses, and a new quay had to be built in front of them for this purpose.

The import of coal from Northumberland and Durham, and its export both to London and abroad, continued in the 18th century, as did the wine trade, but the latter declined in the 19th century. Fishing was also important; a few whaling vessels worked off Greenland.

The early 19th century saw many improvements in Lynn: the streets were paved and drained and gas lighting was installed. It is not surprising that such a prosperous town should have been able to support two busy weekly markets which brought farmers and gentry into town. Many fine inns catered for their needs, and there was a variety of shops and entertainments available.

In 1722 Defoe considered Yarmouth better built than Norwich, although restricted by its site:

> Had they a larger space within the gates, there would before now have been many spacious streets of note and fine buildings erected ... The ships ride so close that for half a mile together they go across the stream with their bowsprits over the land ... so that one may walk from ship to ship as on a floating bridge all along the shore side.

Trade consisted of wool for Holland, barley for London, and coal and fish, both herring and white fish.

An early 18th-century map of Yarmouth shows, in 34 little drawings in the borders, a selection of the many fine pieces of architecture in the town. St George's Chapel, one of the few Renaissance ecclesiastical buildings in East Anglia, was built in 1714. Other notable structures were the new town hall, built in a classical style which harmonised with the wealthy merchants' houses on the quay; the new vicarage built by the Corporation; the late 17th-century Customs House and the attractive Fishermen's Hospital founded in 1702.

The annual Herring Fair was still the most important event in the calendar for Yarmouth. According to Defoe, the fair meant 'the land was covered with people, and the river with barques and boats'. Barrels of salted herrings were traded to Italy, Spain, Portugal and Russia.

By the end of the 18th century Yarmouth had become a fashionable watering place; its bracing climate was recommended by doctors. The

118 *Horatio, Lord Nelson, 1758-1805.*

area of sandy heath known as the Denes had been largely undeveloped except for a few windmills, because the wealthy tradesmen who controlled the town corporation feared competition from a new commercial area outside the walls. The first building here was an army barracks during the Napoleonic Wars; the officers organised horse racing from 1810, which greatly enhanced the fashionable reputation of the town. The most impressive structure on the Denes in the early 19th century was the Nelson column, built to commemorate Norfolk's most famous sailor, born in Burnham Thorpe and a frequent visitor to Yarmouth, between 1815 and 1817.

Other changes were taking place in Yarmouth apart from the development of tourism. Port activities were becoming less diversified with an increased reliance on coal, corn, and fishing, with milling also becoming more important. The population doubled between 1801 and 1851, and at last there was expansion outside the walls. Instead of the narrow 'rows' houses were built around large courtyards known as 'bleaches' where washing could be hung, some of which still survive.

Norwich, Lynn and Yarmouth retained their pre-eminence throughout the period, but many other smaller market towns prospered and had a key role in the business and commercial life of their districts. The increasing significance of Quarter Sessions and the work of J.P.s in Tudor times meant that the towns in which they were held flourished. Wymondham, Holt, Acle and Swaffham were all Quarter Sessions towns,

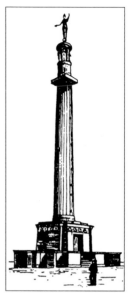

119 *Nelson monument, Great Yarmouth, 1819.*

120 *Fishwharf scene, Great Yarmouth, c.1910.*

while the more important Assizes were held in Thetford, Norwich and Lynn. Although many towns suffered disastrous fires in the 16th and 17th centuries, a good number of Tudor houses survive to remind us of their prosperity.

In 1722, when Defoe visited the eastern counties, Norfolk was still by the standards of the time an industrial area supporting a dense population. In the closely-packed villages of east and mid-Norfolk there was plenty of work even for children, in the spinning and repairing of wool for textiles. These affluent villages provided the goods and livestock for the market towns like Aylsham, Reepham and Holt. The small North Sea ports like Cley, Blakeney and Wells were also enjoying a boom period, exporting grain to Holland and around the coast to London, and importing coal from the north-east. Cley was also renowned for its sea-salt.

Weaving and spinning slowly died out in the countryside, and instead became almost exclusively Norwich-based. Heavy goods and livestock were difficult to transport by road, and so the local agricultural markets continued to thrive; the many fine Georgian market places that survive (as at Hingham), only superficially spoilt by modern shop fronts, are evidence of this. Many attractive architectural reminders of those days can still be seen today, as at Swaffham, whose elegant Butter Cross enhances the Georgian atmosphere of the still busy market place, and reminds us of the important butter trade. From the late 1840s agricultural wealth often expressed itself by the erection of a corn hall. Previously corn merchants had met farmers in pubs; but now they paid for the right to a stand in the new hall, where, seated behind high desks, they examined the grain samples brought them by the farmers. The useful life of some of these halls was rather short, with the decline in the corn trade after the 1870s. They were used for public meetings and eventually some as at Dereham and Fakenham became cinemas or bingo halls.

121 *Norfolk population changes.*

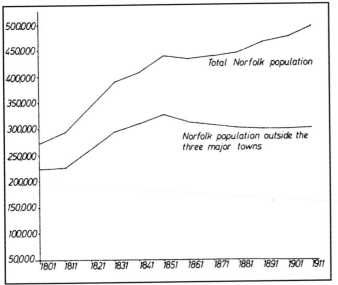
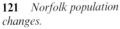

Early 18th-century towns often had reputations as dirty, unpleasant and unsafe places, and it was realised that this could affect trade. Great efforts were made to pave streets, erect lighting, and control 'nuisances' like the depositing of rubbish in the road. Before 1737, Dereham was said to be the dirtiest town in Norfolk, whereas by the early 19th century it was described as the most 'improving'. Most towns had a police station by 1840, a gas works by 1850 and a water works by 1900.

All market towns had their tailors, hatters, cobblers and watchmakers. Horses were needed for transport as well as for farm work, so there were also saddlers, harness makers and

KEY

1. Post mill and miller's house
2. Hill House
3. Assembly Rooms (built 1756)
4. The Shambles
5. The old pound, Norwich Street (demolished 1770)
6. The Guild Hall
7. The rector's tythe barn

Inns with bush hanging outside as a sign

8. *The George*
9. *The Eagle*
10. *The King's Arms*
11. *Lord Nelson*
12. *The King's Head*
13. *The Bull*
14. *The Swan*
15. *The Rose*
16. *The Green Man*
17. Demolished inn in Guildhall Row
18. *The Duke of York*
19. *The Antelope*
20. *The Chequers*

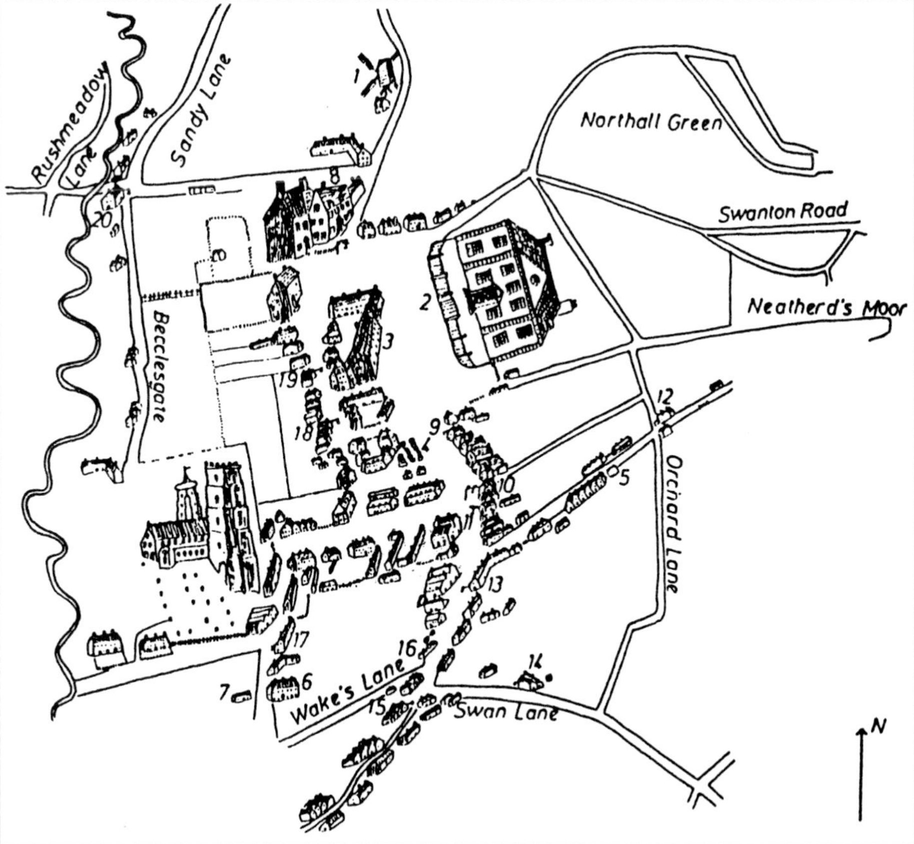

122 *Dereham in the late 1750s, (Orchard Lane is now Commercial Road and Swan Lane is now London Road).*

blacksmiths. Basket makers provided essential containers for harvesting and carrying animal feed. Brewing and malting steadily expanded. Other services were provided in the towns by banks, lawyers and surgeons.

As the importance of local weaving declined and the production of agricultural goods increased, wealthy farmers had more to sell and more to spend, in the pubs, on horse racing and cock fighting. The open heath at Swaffham provided an ideal racetrack, and other sites were found at Dereham and at Mousehold Heath near Norwich, where there was also a fashionable carriage drive. Theatres and assembly rooms were built in a number of towns. At Dereham theatrical performances took place regularly from 1749, although the theatre itself was not built until 1812. Most towns had libraries and reading rooms where the London papers were also available.

Alongside the old market towns an entirely new type of settlement was beginning to appear—the seaside resorts. The small fishing village of Cromer was visited from about 1785 by 'two or three families of retired habits whose favourable reports soon attracted others'. It soon became a highly fashionable sea-bathing centre, with a daily coach from Norwich via Aylsham. By 1850 five large hotels had been built, and many boarding-houses. One continuing problem was the cliff erosion; a

123 *Fakenham Corn Hall, from a 19th century engraving.*

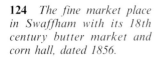
124 *The fine market place in Swaffham with its 18th century butter market and corn hall, dated 1856.*

125 *Cromer in the early 19th century, oil painting by James Stark, 1837.*

bath-house with reading and billiard rooms was erected in 1814 and washed away in 1836. Nevertheless, the population doubled between 1801 and 1851 and continued to rise thereafter when many other small towns declined. Although fishing remained important, and there was some coastal trade in coal and agricultural goods, tourism was now by far Cromer's most important industry.

The development of both small and large towns was greatly influenced by the improved communications of the 18th and 19th centuries. One of the first turnpike acts in England was for part of the present Norwich-London road (the A11), between Wymondham and Attleborough, in 1695. However, the turnpike movement as a whole came rather later to Norfolk than to other parts of England. Roads were not under such pressure as those in newly industrialised regions, and many, especially in west Norfolk, traversed light well-drained soils where the problems of maintenance were not too great. The majority of Norfolk turnpikes were set up after 1770, but some main roads (such as the present A1068, the Fakenham to Brandon road) were never turnpiked at all, whilst others were only in part. Some market towns remained unaffected, and others benefited from increased traffic.

The same can be said of the introduction of stage coaches in the late 18th and early 19th centuries. Where possible, they kept to the improved

126 *Norfolk market towns in the toll road age.*

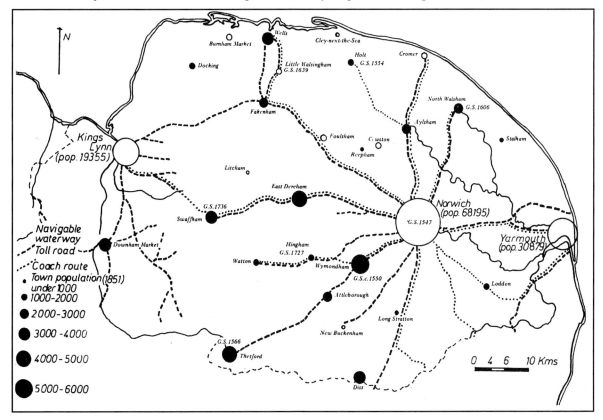

127 *A Norfolk wherry.*

turnpike roads, where speeds of up to ten miles an hour could be maintained, a factor which accentuated the differences between well- and poorly-placed market towns. Norwich was the obvious focus of local services. There were also daily coaches to Lynn, stopping at Swaffham and Dereham, and Yarmouth via Acle and Loddon. Other towns were served twice or three times a week, one of these visits being timed to coincide with market day.

Even before the advent of the stage coach, travellers needed to stop and refresh themselves and their horses. Towns on major through-routes, such as Wymondham, Attleborough and Thetford on the London road, Dereham and Swaffham on the King's Lynn road, and Diss on the Ipswich road all grew in importance for this reason. The increased traffic generated by the stage coaches produced much work for local wheelwrights, farriers and blacksmiths, as well as a need for increased stabling. Several of the larger towns had coach makers. This period of coach travel has left its monuments in the form of a large number of big coaching inns, usually with huge areas of stabling and yards behind them.

As road transport did not provide a satisfactory method of moving bulky goods, the 18th century relied heavily on water transport, which, if slow and often circuitous, was cheap. River navigation was improved; by 1750 the Nar was navigable to Narborough, where a maltings grew up to process malt before export. This was also a site for the unloading of coal for Dereham and Swaffham. The Little Ouse was navigable as far as Thetford, which again encouraged industrial development. Wherries could take goods from Yarmouth as far as Norwich and water transport was by far the easiest route between the two towns before the opening of the Acle New Road in the 1830s. In 1773 an Act of Parliament was passed to extend the navigable waterway of the Bure from Coltishall as far as Aylsham. Work was finished by 1779 and this brought much business in coal, corn and timber, as well as boat-building and stone masonry, to a new suburb at Millgate.

The traffic generated in an agricultural county was not enough to justify the expense of building canals. However, in 1812 an Act was passed to build a canal from North Walsham to the river Ant at Dilham. The canal was eight miles long, cost £32,000 to build, and was not opened until 1826. It was narrow, only capable of taking boats up to 12 tons. It was never very profitable. The only other attempt to build a canal in Norfolk was the Norwich and Lowestoft Navigation, built to by-pass Yarmouth, which opened in 1833. It had a very short life, as it was taken over by the railway in 1846. The original canal basin was filled in and is now the car park in front of Thorpe Station. On the eve of the arrival of the railways, Norfolk could boast an impressive network of market towns throughout the county, in addition to its three major centres at Norwich, Lynn and Yarmouth.

8

Education

As the general level of prosperity amongst local gentry and farmers increased, there was a greater demand for education in the 16th century. Endowed grammar schools were founded by local benefactors, which provided education on a daily basis for town boys whilst boarders came from further afield. Where a school gained a good reputation, it might change from being a grammar school to become a public school of national repute, as was the case with Gresham's School in Holt.

The 18th and 19th centuries saw the provision of education develop from a very limited number of schools to a highly ordered national system; by 1900 compulsory education was an accepted fact and illiteracy had largely disappeared. The reasons for the increased interest in education were many. In the period of unrest which followed the French Revolution, the English upper classes realised the need to control the power of the mob. An educational system was needed which would teach children the Christian duty of obedience, as well as to read and write. At the same time, there was increasing clamour for an extension of the franchise. It was realised that a voting nation should be a literate one; also, that the workers needed to operate the new industrial machines would have to be better educated. These reasons, however, were secondary to the main aim of producing God-fearing, law-abiding, obedient citizens.

The most difficult schools to trace, although they probably offered the only chance an 18th-century village child had of schooling, are the 'dame schools'. A 'school' might consist of ten or twelve children in a back room, with perhaps a shop at the front and the 'schoolmaster' dividing his time between the two. Very often little more than babysitting facilities were provided. There was no inspection of premises, or any examination of the master or mistress's fitness to teach. Teachers were often cripples or elderly persons who could not cope with manual work. The limited remuneration offered by teaching the children of the poor could not attract teachers of ability. Some 'dame schools' were probably in existence for only a few years; the report of the 1834 Parliamentary Select Committee lists a surprising number of schools for Norfolk, but it is probable that many of these were short-lived 'dame schools'. Three fee-paying daily schools existed in Acle, and two in each of the small parishes of Alborough and Aldeby.

128 *A desk from Rocklands National school, 1851.*

97

129 *Saxon carving from Thetford grammar school.*

It was obvious that these schools were far from adequate: also, even their modest fees placed them out of reach for many. During the 18th century charitable persons left private endowments to set up schools for the poor. By 1816 there were 100 endowed rural schools in Norfolk, catering for 3,500 children, like that at Wighton, for which Sarah Charles left money to teach six girls to read, knit, sew and learn their catechism. The terms of endowment often stipulated that the children should learn some useful work. In 1718, Mrs. Anne Neve left £200 for the support of a schoolmistress to 'teach 28 or more poor children of Ringland to read and (needle) work'. The distribution of such schools was very patchy, and they could in no way provide mass education.

Sunday schools began in the late 18th century, originally for children who worked during the week. As they spread to rural areas, a secondary aim became that of preventing hooliganism, which often took place on Sundays. In Fakenham there were four Sunday schools by 1834, one run by the Church of England, one by the Wesleyans, one by the Independents and one by the Particular Baptists. Tuition was nearly always free, and often provided by the lady of the manor or the vicar's wife. Their main purpose was to teach children to read the Bible, and attendance at church or chapel was part of the school day.

The immensity of the problem on a national scale led to the setting-up of two religious societies for the promotion of education. The National Society for promoting the Education of the Poor was founded in 1811, and the British and Foreign School Society in 1814. The National Society was closely linked to the Church of England and the British Society to the nonconformist, particularly Independent, churches. These religious differences led to continual rivalry. Naturally, religious education played an important part in the curriculum of all the schools established by these societies. The National Society quickly set up schools in Norfolk, while the British Society made slower progress. By 1816 the Select Committee on Education estimated that just over 26,000 children in Norfolk attended school, 8,500 of these on Sunday only.

By 1840, 64 new schools had been built and the number of children attending had doubled. In many cases the school was first erected by a landowner or rector; in others the school did not have its own building, but used churches, chapels or private houses. The predominance of the National Society meant that the children of dissenters could have problems in obtaining education. The 1834 Select Committee on Education decided that standards in country schools were generally lower than in urban areas, partly because children were usually at school for a shorter time. The low wages paid to teachers meant they spent time supplementing their income with other work. In spite of the realisation of the importance

130 *Carrow school, Norwich.*

131 *The interior of Carrow school.*

of education in general, and of regular schooling in particular, it was still felt that compulsory education was neither desirable nor practical. 147 Norfolk villages were still without any school.

In 1858 the Rev. Hedley was the Educational Commissioner responsible for studying a sample area which included part of the fens and Breckland in Lincolnshire, Cambridgeshire and the Norfolk areas of Downham and Thetford. He wrote:

> I was repeatedly told that children above the age of eight were away from school for entire intervals varying from four to eight months and that those above 10 to 11 were frequently only to be found at school for a few weeks in the winter ... Teachers can usually do no more than bring the children up again each winter to the point which they had reached before. Children begin to leave school finally at the age of nine.

The main reason for this lax attendance was the amount of field work available. Fruit and vegetable picking, stone picking and other tasks were the usual excuses. At certain times all hands were needed, and some families near the poverty line depended on the extra money earned by children.

From 1833 a grant of £20,000 per annum provided a fund from which government grants could be made for building purposes, so long as half the necessary money was raised locally. This had the disadvantage of encouraging school building in the richer areas. In 1839, the amount available was increased to £30,000. In 1870 the Forster Education Act ordered the setting up of board schools where there were not enough voluntary schools. The resulting network should have meant enough schools to make education compulsory, and indeed local boards were empowered to do this if they wished, but not until 1886 were there actually enough school places available for all children. From 1876, however, parents were compelled to see that their offspring had education. By 1880 72 board schools had been set up in Norfolk. Sometimes existing schools were handed over to the boards, but more often new ones had to be built.

Although the part played by the state in education had increased considerably, it was still a subsidiary role in rural Norfolk. The 72 board schools were outnumbered by 126 National and 115 voluntary schools. Very few rural schools had been set up by the British Society, largely because the expense was often beyond a village nonconformist congregation. They were mostly confined to towns such as Dereham (1841), North Walsham and Wells (1838) and Cley (1860). To meet the shortage of trained teachers needed for this expansion of school provision, an institute for teacher training was set up in the Cathedral close in Norwich, becoming the Norwich Training College. It moved to Keswick on the city outskirts after the Second World War.

Compulsory education was extremely difficult to enforce. There were not enough attendance officers, and when they did report parents to the magistrate, the latter was often one of the farmer J.P.s who were responsible for providing employment for children. The attendance officers were not respected. In October 1877, when one visited North Elmham school, all the children whom he called up and warned because of their irregular attendance stayed away with their brothers and sisters for the rest of the week. George Baldry tells us in *The Rabbit Skin Cap* that he went to school for the first time in June 1871, when he was six and a half, but the next summer he started work at a brick kiln. By the end of the century, however, most children were at school until they were twelve.

As well as paid employment, the weather often prevented children attending. Gales, deep snow, hard frost and floods were real obstacles for children who had to walk up to four miles to school, but the head-master at North Elmham did not always consider these excuses valid. In November 1897 he wrote in the log book, 'Great storm. Only 68 present in the morning. Weather considered too bad to send children to school, but not too bad for some to go gathering fallen branches'. Another reason for absence was simply the attraction of local functions: sporting events such as cricket matches took children out of school as well as agricultural shows, fairs and auctions.

132 *Pupils outside Swannington school, 1903.*

133 *A potential scholar,*
c.1880.

The gentry often felt it their duty to provide for their tenants' well-being. The extent of this paternalism varied greatly, but often included school building or church restoration. Often the local landowner built schools which were then vested in the National Society. Of the 115 voluntary schools in 1880, 64 had been erected by landowners and about twenty were still entirely supported by them. Some took a great deal of interest after they were built. The school log books at Felthorpe show that the Hon. and Mrs. E. Fellowes visited the school they had built in 1846 at least once a week in the 1870s. Other gentry provided schools but did not maintain them. This was done by a voluntary rate, and by small fees of between 1d. and 3d., sometimes less for the second and third children in a family. The lofty rooms may have been impressive and airy, but they were impossible to heat; log books speak of children sent home when it was too cold to write. Desks and benches were arranged in rows. The open space in front of the desks was used to hear children read or recite. Windows were usually too high for the children to see out, and despite their sometimes ornate exteriors, most schools were austere and comfortless inside. Many had no water either for drinking or washing, and lavatories were inadequate and insanitary; a fact shown up by the frequency with which schools were closed by sanitary inspectors following epidemics. The dreary daily routine was reinforced by corporal punishment.

As the century wore on, the curriculum became broader, with history and geography being taught to the older children. Reading, writing, arithmetic, and religious education, with formal physical education, formed the main part of teaching. However, there were school treats. At Elmham skating on the lake was sometimes allowed. Magic lantern shows and other entertainments such as a ventriloquist's or magician's visit might be arranged. The school patron or the rector might give presents at Christmas and a summer tea party in his grounds. Most schools closed for a month or six weeks at harvest time and also at Christmas, Easter and Whitsun, and extra holidays might be granted if a special event occurred in the neighbourhood.

Education finished at twelve. Despite the restrictive curriculum, many gained a taste for reading. Some schoolmasters ran adult evening classes, and the 1834 Select Committee reported that 45 Norfolk villages had lending libraries attached to the school. The second half of the 19th century saw the building of reading rooms in some villages, like that at Holkham, built to celebrate Queen Victoria's Silver Jubilee. Sometimes 'literary institutes' met in private houses, but little is known of these, or of the books discussed. Servants in some great houses were encouraged to read books from a 'servants' library'. At Blickling this library contained religious works, books of legends, and biographies of exemplary people.

Education in the 19th century produced men and women with an interest in learning, who continued to read and study after leaving school and became an educated and articulate working-class group, in the struggle to improve living standards.

9

Church and Chapel

In the early 18th century, England was not generally a religious nation. The Anglican church still dominated religious activities, but expansion and change were hampered by its outdated organisation. The distribution of churches reflected the medieval population pattern; large churches were now surrounded by only a few cottages. The evils of non-residence (where clergymen did not actually reside in their livings), of plurality (the holding of more than one benefice) and nepotism (the granting of livings to members of the patron's family) had not been removed by the Reformation. Although the majority of 18th-century clerics probably only held one living, at least 100 Norfolk clergymen had two, and Nelson's father an exceptional seven. A single living was often too poor to support a vicar; in 1809 160 parishes provided benefices worth less than £150 per annum, the minimum at which a 'middle-class' living standard could be maintained. Non-residence was an even greater problem. Very few parishes had a rectory, and those which existed were often considered unfit to live in. Some vicars held other positions which entitled them to live elsewhere, like the vicar of Redenhall who was resident chaplain to the British merchants of Oporto, Portugal. The practice of presenting livings to sons, brothers or other near relations was widespread. Sir R. Kemp was patron of both Florden and Gissing in the 1730s, and gave them both to his younger son Thomas.

In 18th-century Norfolk the bishops gave little effective leadership. Some held the position for less than two years and others were non-resident with little influence over their clergy.

The diaries of Parson Woodforde, vicar of Weston Longville from 1776-1803, portray the life of a typical country parson, with more in common with the leisured classes than with his humble parishioners. He carried out his parochial duties in accordance with the standards of the time, giving Christmas lunch to the poor and paying doctor's fees for those who could not afford them. His only innovation was the introduction of Good Friday prayers. He seems little concerned by the activities of religious groups such as the Methodists.

Alongside the Anglican church were those of the nonconformists—the Independents, Quakers and Baptists who had broken away from the

134 *The Rev. James Woodforde.*

135 *A 15th-century roof boss in the nave of Norwich Cathedral showing the jaws of Hell.*

Church of England. In 1717 there were 20 Congregationalist and four Baptist churches in Norfolk, mostly in towns. As well as congregations in Norwich, Yarmouth and Lynn, there were also groups in Wymondham, New Buckenham, Tunstead, Armingland, Bradfield, Denton, Colkirk, Filby, Guestwick, Long Stratton, and Hapton. The 18th century saw stagnation in dissenting as well as established religion. A few new chapels were built, but the dissenters were mostly closely-knit isolated communities who had little impact on the established church.

The arrival of the Wesleyans in the second half of the century did arouse the church, leading in many cases to mob violence and attacks on the preachers. John Wesley, who travelled all over England preaching, first visited Norwich in 1745 and had made over forty visits to Norfolk by 1790. Much of the work of conversion, however, was due not to him but to his lay preachers who sometimes, as with the Calvinistic Methodists at the Tabernacle in Norwich, broke away from his original teachings.

Wesley first visited Yarmouth in 1754, but a house was not licensed for preaching until 1772. A chapel was built in 1783. He visited King's Lynn in 1771 and a chapel opened in 1786. Wherever he went he left a small band of believers who went out to set up groups or 'classes' in surrounding villages, which were grouped into 'circuits' based on a central chapel, usually in a town. The Norwich circuit was set up in 1765 and the Lynn circuit in 1776. In 1786 the Yarmouth circuit was separated from the parent Norwich one and by 1800 there were seven circuits, the others being Diss (1790), Walsingham (1791), Thetford (1797) and Framlingham (1799).

Except in towns, few groups had their own chapels, meeting instead in private houses or other buildings licensed for preaching. Methodists were instructed to attend their parish churches for communion, but they were not always welcome. By 1800 there were probably about seventy-five villages with licensed Methodist meeting-places. This made them numerically far more important than the earlier nonconformist sects, and their linked structure made them far more of a potential threat to the Church of England. However, after Wesley's death in 1791, the leadership became increasingly autocratic and factions developed. The general policy seems to have been to concentrate efforts in the growing industrial towns, yet even in rural Norfolk travelling Wesleyan preachers provided plain sermons aimed at the needs of the poor. If some of the initial fervour had gone out of the movement by 1800, seeds had been sown which would germinate and grow, particularly with the coming of the Primitive Methodists in the 19th century.

The religious revival of the 19th century is one of the most striking developments of the period. The evangelical movement within the Church of England showed itself most obviously in the work of the Clapham sect, centred round the vicar of Clapham in London, John Venn, who went there from Little Dunham, Norfolk, in 1792. He gathered round him a group of influential men who lived austerely and practised philanthropy. The Oxford Movement which developed from this was an

136 *Relief, in Norwich Cathedral, showing a Norman bishop, possibly Losinga.*

academic, clerical and conservative movement which advocated 'high church' ritual and theological debate. By the mid-century its influence had filtered down to country churches which replaced parish orchestras by organs and introduced surpliced choirs, changes originally regarded with suspicion but ultimately accepted.

The Oxford Movement also advocated church restoration. Ladbrooke's illustrations of Norfolk churches about 1800 show many in a ruinous state, and even in 1851 West Lexham was described as a very small parish where 'the church is in a wretched condition'. In 1884 the Rev. Jessop of Scarning could report that between 1840 and 1879 'upwards of 860 churches have been built or put into a condition of complete repair at a cost of £900,000'.

The last of the old school of Norwich prelates was Bishop Bathurst (1806-37). His successor, Edward Stanley, carried out regular visitations and steadily reduced non-residency, mainly by building rectories. By 1842, 68 had been built and 200 appeared by 1900. Some were small, like that at Flitcham, with only three bedrooms and two reception rooms; others, such as that at East Bilney (1837), were far larger.

137 *The Rev. Benjamin John Armstrong.*

We can follow some of these changes through the diaries of the Rev. Armstrong, vicar of Dereham from 1850 to 1888, which describe a life in some ways similar, in others very different, from that of Parson Woodforde. Both had a tranquil existence with plenty of time for social gatherings and visits to the local gentry. However, the Anglican church in Dereham was more dynamic as a result of Armstrong's ministry, and it is here that the difference between him and Woodforde lies. Rev. Armstrong was very concerned with parish matters and played a leading role in any charitable organisation in Dereham. He reorganised the form of the church services and introduced new ones. By the time of his death the parish church was a major religious force in the town. Throughout his ministry, Armstrong was well aware of the local dissenters, noting in his diary for one Sunday in 1861 'Afternoon congregation much thinned by a great "camp meeting" and "love feast" got up by dissenters'.

The number of Methodist chapels in Norfolk had grown between 1800 and 1850, but expansion was slower than in the initial period of evangelism. Thirty more houses were licensed for preaching by 1820. Chapels were built by groups who had raised enough money. The small group at Themelthorpe is typical of many: they did not begin to raise money for their chapel until 1889, although there had been Methodists in the parish since 1811.

Many groups split away from the main Methodist body. By 1851, there were the New Connexion, the Bible Christians, the Wesleyan Methodists Association, the Wesleyan Reformers and the most important group, the Primitive Methodists. This latter group had a working-class leadership, as well as membership. The movement entered Norfolk from the north, reaching Newark in 1817 and King's Lynn in 1821. A group had been set up in the latter by 1823, as also in Fakenham and Norwich. By 1836 there were groups in most market towns from where preachers

138 *Bawdeswell church, rebuilt 1955.*

139 *St Peter Mancroft church, Norwich.*

went into the countryside. By 1851 there were 234 chapels in Norfolk with over 25,000 members. This compared with the membership of all other Wesleyan groups of over 42,000 divided amongst 260 chapels.

A national survey of church attendance was undertaken on Sunday 30 March 1851, which showed that the proportion of the Norfolk population going to a place of worship was higher than the national average. Nearly two-thirds attended at least one service. However, in common with the rest of England, worshippers were almost equally divided between Anglican and nonconformist churches. The largest sect was the Methodists, who accounted for an attendance of 89,930, nearly half of whom were Primitives. The Baptists attracted 23,865 worshippers and the Independents 14,742. The other sects were all much smaller. Roman Catholics formed 0.3 per cent only; many other counties had over one per cent.

Something of the religious life of the three market towns of Dereham, Swaffham and North Walsham is revealed to us by the *Norfolk News*, which in 1865-6 ran a series of articles entitled 'Sundays in the Country'. In North Walsham the reporter found the service in the parish church dull; the vicar 'took more interest in church restoration than in inspiring his flock'. The Primitive Methodist service was much more lively, 'nobody asleep there'. The Wesleyan Methodists lacked the Primitives' enthusiasm. The chapel was not half full and many arrived late. The Independents were flourishing, with two Sunday and one weekday service, a library and a clothing club.

The vicar of Swaffham provided three services on Sunday and two daily services in the week. He was involved in 'charitable works which are very scarce amongst the dissenters'. The Baptists had a congregation of about three hundred, but the Wesleyans no more lively than those in North Walsham. The Primitive congregation was small but enthusiastic.

In Dereham there were five dissenting chapels as well as the parish church. The Primitive Methodist chapel was well attended. The Methodist Free church service was taken in a simple fashion with many interruptions from the congregation. The reporter found the Rev. Armstrong's service well attended and the church doing much good work. To the modern reader, perhaps the most surprising thing is the very large congregations attracted.

140 *A 15th-century bench end from St Nicholas' Chapel, King's Lynn.*

Norfolk vicars were asked in the 'articles of enquiry' sent out before a visitation from the bishop whether they felt that Sundays were observed with greater or lesser decorum than previously. Invariably they replied that observance was greater by the mid-century. A lady brought up in Saxlingham in the 1890s remembers Sundays: she went to church three times and was only allowed to read the Bible or *Pilgrim's Progress*. 'Saturday nights, the work basket, knitting and sewing, with the weekly newspaper folded on top were all put in the cupboard till Monday'.

The Primitive Methodists continued to expand, particularly into remote areas where the agricultural labourers were willing converts. In 1872 the Norfolk Primitive membership was twice that of the Wesleyan.

141 Above. *The Octagon chapel in Norwich, 1754-6.*

142 Above right. *The Mariners' chapel, Great Yarmouth.*

The membership of both groups rose slightly by 1890. This rise is more significant when we realise that rural population was falling.

A hundred years previously the church had impinged very little on the lives of ordinary people, except at baptism, marriage and burial. The vicar was a remote person, perhaps not even living in the parish, and the church uncared for. Both Anglicanism and nonconformity had changed by the 1850s. The Sunday school and the Sunday treat were part of village life, and nonconformist camp meetings, when 'preachers spoke from waggons in a meadow and there was great singing' were enjoyed by many. The parish church was now closely involved in local charitable activities, with the vicar and probably his family taking a leading role. By 1900 the 'Victorian Sunday' and daily family prayers were an established part of middle-class life. That religion played a more obvious part in daily life in 1900 than in 1800 cannot be doubted, but whether the average man had a more profound understanding of the things of the spirit is a question which cannot be answered.

10

The Coming of the Railways

The first Norfolk railway was opened in 1844 between Norwich and Yarmouth. Within a year the long-awaited connection to London was finished. By 1850, lines to Ipswich, Fakenham and King's Lynn through Dereham and Swaffham were completed. The railway brought many changes. Travel became not only much faster, but also cheaper, for goods and passengers. For the first time small villages along the main routes had direct access to London, as well as Norwich. In spite of higher London prices, fatstock had often been sold locally because several days were needed to drive sheep to London. They lost as much as seven pounds; a bullock could lose 28 pounds on the journey. After the opening of the railway, fatstock could reach London within a day with virtually no weight loss. This was a boon for livestock farmers, although a blow for some local fatstock markets.

Fast cheap transport was particularly important for perishable goods. Fish could be taken fresh from Yarmouth to London, and dairy farming also received a boost from the opening up of large urban markets.

The cost of inland transport had made coal expensive away from ports; it was 18s. a ton in King's Lynn and 30s. in Dereham before the railway age, which brought the price down to 15s. in the 1850s. However, the volume of coastal coal traffic was greatly reduced: although hazardous and laborious, it had been important for both Lynn and Yarmouth.

143 *Lord Hastings' waiting room, Melton Constable.*

The first casualties of the railway age were the stage coaches, most of which finished running on rail routes within a year. The coaching inns along these roads declined, although the importance of local carriers and coaches in areas outside the railway network remained. Instead of coaching inns, there were now railway hotels.

Towns were greatly affected by their position on, or away from, a railway line. Dereham, on the junction of the London to Fakenham, and the Yarmouth to Lynn routes, grew rapidly, and a new industrial area developed near the station.

Swaffham had been on a crossroads in the coaching era and prospered accordingly; it was now only a station on a through route, and went into decline.

The principal effect of railways on Norfolk was the beginning of mass tourism. 'We may perhaps date the beginning of Yarmouth's role in this market from the special day trip of 30 June 1846, when school children from Norwich, Wymondham and Attleborough were conveyed to Yarmouth by rail for 3d'. In 1841 the Victoria Building Company had commenced building operations on the Denes; over the next 20 years rows of substantial terraces appeared to accommodate Yarmouth's visitors—Brandon, Kimberley, Albert and Britannia Terraces amongst them. The Wellington Pier Company was established in 1853 and the pier with its fine promenades was built the following year. In 1875, an aquarium, winter garden and concert room beside the pier added to existing attractions, and Yarmouth had become well-established as one of England's most flourishing resorts.

144 *Norfolk market towns after the coming of the railways. (The arrows show whether the population rose or fell 1851-91.)*

Although much of the port's costal traffic had vanished with the coming of the railways, lighters and wherries still carried coal, fertilizers and cattle cake inland as far as Aylsham, North Walsham, Beccles and Bungay, and brought grain back. Much of the barley was used in the very extensive maltings in the town, and the malt was then used locally or sent to London. The importance of the herring and mackerel fishery increased

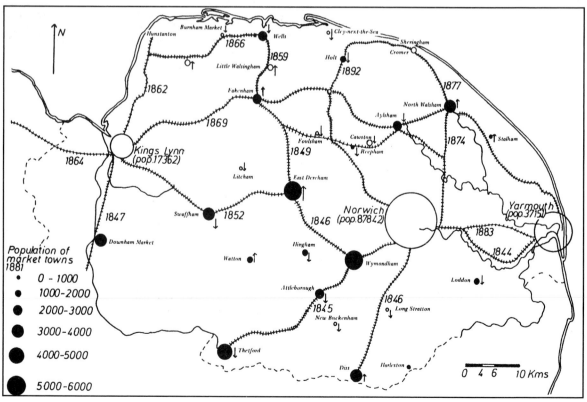

as other traffic declined; in 1852 900 tons of fish left Yarmouth by rail. Mackerel fishing began in early May and lasted about ten weeks. It employed about a hundred boats and 1,400 men and women in the 1850s. The railway provided a new national market; the value of the mackerel fishery went up from £14,500 in 1841 to over £200,000 by 1852. Herring fishing began in September, again lasting about ten weeks. Two hundred Yarmouth boats and many others from north-eastern coastal ports were involved, and often as many as 26,000 fish were caught by one boat. Most of the catch was salted and cured in the many curing houses. In the 1850s about 35,000 barrels of herring were exported, mostly to Russia, and almost twice as many sold within Britain. By 1911 export figures had increased to 330,000 barrels. Thereafter trade was disrupted by the First World War and the profitable Russian market was lost. The fisheries and their associ-

ated industries, such as basketmaking and netmaking, employed about 5,000 by the mid-century. A new covered fish wharf was constructed on the South Denes in 1869, which had to be enlarged in 1902.

145 *Fish curing houses, Great Yarmouth.*

Lynn also suffered from the loss of coastal and inland traffic to railway competition. The number of vessels registered at the Customs House dropped from 122 in 1835 to 79 in 1880, and the population fell between 1851-81 by 2,000 to just over 17,000. Exports became limited to a small range of agricultural goods and silica sand from the Leziate sand pits, and imports consisted of coal and oil cake. New docks were dug in the late 1860s in an effort to increase trade. The Alexandra Dock was opened in 1869; 165 vessels used it that year, but by 1880 over five hundred and eighty called there. It was extended between 1881-4 and the Bentinck Dock was constructed. Both docks were connected to the railway and trade revived somewhat by the end of the century. A small fishing fleet continued to operate, employing just under four hundred men and boys. Various port industries based on agriculture developed; maltings, breweries, corn mills and seed crushers.

The railways brought a temporary improvement in the fortunes of the Norwich cloth trade, as coal was cheaper. New machinery was installed. The Jacquard loom, where the pattern is governed by a series

146 *View across the port of King's Lynn, with the Purfleet and Customs House in the foreground.*

of punched cards, came into more general use and shawl production was at its peak in the 1850s. However, the fashion for them declined in the 1870s and the manufacture of crêpe increased to provide for an ever-increasing demand for elaborate mourning dresses. The largest crêpe manufacturer was John Grant, who also had factories in Yarmouth, North Walsham and Bungay.

Other industries appeared. Jeremiah Colman moved his mustard factory from Stoke Holy Cross into Norwich in 1854, partly because of the cheap labour supply. By 1880, he employed 2,500 people. He chose a site near both the river and the railway for convenient transport, and soon started to manufacture starch and laundry blue as well as mustard. Colman took a very paternalistic attitude to his workforce, setting up a school in 1857 and a dispensary in 1864, soon after appointing the first industrial nurse in England. He became a leading Norwich figure and was Lord Mayor in 1868. From 1871-95 he was M.P. for Norwich, taking over a traditional gentry role.

The manufacture of agricultural machinery became a major Norwich industry. The firm of Barnard, Bishop and Barnard, famous for their invention of the wire netting machine, whose product was in great demand

XI *Sandringham House and gardens.*

XII *Blickling Hall with the lake behind and church in the foreground. Blickling Hall and park is owned by the National Trust and open to the public.*

in America for fencing the prairies, were also admired for the quality of their decorative ironwork, one of their best-known pieces being the Norwich gates at Sandringham. By 1854 there were seven other agricultural machine makers in Norwich.

By far the largest employers, however, were the boot and shoe manufacturers, of whom there were 220 firms by 1854. Their employees increased in number from 1,912 in 1841 to 6,278 in 1861 and about 8,500 in 1881, supplying goods for export and the home market. Other expanding industries included breweries, vinegar works, tanneries and soaperies, using the raw materials from local agriculture, and chemical works, oil cake and artificial manure manufacturers, serving farmers' needs. The railway brought more people into the city to do business and in 1861 a new Corn Hall was built, larger than its predecessor.

The continuing importance of the river as a means of transport is shown by the fact that as late as 1880 nearly all the major industrial sites were along its banks. Going north from the Carrow Works, the banks were lined with malt houses and breweries. The area by the cathedral was still open, but as the river curved to the west, factories were to be found on both sides of it, including dye works, timber yards, a corn mill, iron works and crêpe factories.

Jarrold's became Norwich's first department store when its London Street premises opened in 1840. At first they concentrated on bookselling,

147 *Work with sifting frames and stampers in Colman's mustard factory, c.1900.*

printing and patent medicines, but by the 1880s had extended their range to leather and travel goods, sports equipment and silverware, and branches were opened in Cromer (1881), Yarmouth (1888) and Sheringham (1896).

Norwich's population increased rapidly from 1850, but the decline in the woollen industry meant much unemployment. Areas of slum housing developed; the poor conditions were brought to public attention by a cholera epidemic in 1850. During the second half of the century the population of several central parishes declined, and new terraces of working-class housing were built in the suburbs. The introduction of horse-trams in 1879 and electric ones in 1900 made it easier for people to live further from their work. The poorest new developments were between Ber Street and the river, and there was equally dense housing in the Peafields area of Lakenham. The most spacious new housing appeared around the Ipswich and Newmarket roads, while a middle sort of development was found along the Unthank road and the adjoining streets.

From the 1870s great improvements were made in the city. Piped filtered water was available from 1850 when the Water Company was founded, but drainage did not appear until 1870. In 1880 Chapel Field Gardens were laid out and in 1881 electric lighting was introduced. Certainly, by 1900 Norwich was a cleaner and pleasanter place than 50 years previously.

The first phase of railway building was over by 1855, and there was little development for another 20 years. Many parts of Norfolk were still a long way from the nearest station, particularly in the north-east. A rural area with declining industry and, after 1850, a declining population, did not generate enough traffic to make the opening of new lines worthwhile. However, one branch line which opened in 1862 showed the existence of a new potential source of passengers. The King's Lynn to Hunstanton line was built, and immediately the landowner Hamon Le Strange began to develop Hunstanton as a holiday resort, for which the potential of the area, with its good beach and fine scenery, was obvious. The population trebled to nearly 2,000 in the 30 years after the building of the railway, and many hotels and boarding houses, as well as a shopping street and private residences sprang up.

In 1874 a line was built from Norwich to North Walsham and in 1877 it was extended to Cromer. The opening of this holiday line meant that the Norfolk side of the Great Eastern Railway's operations began to show a profit. Cromer could now be reached by a larger cross-section of society and its holiday trade grew enormously. 'Hotels of a size and magnificence that make the dwellings on the cliff seem humble in comparison, adorn, perhaps too well, the unpretentious coastline, like jewels on the dress of a simple village maid'. Even then, the amount of development that was desirable was a subject of debate. The respectable residents of Cromer did not want to be inundated with trippers. The *Royal Links* hotel was built in 1887, the *Grand* and *Metropole* hotels in 1890 and the *Hotel de Paris* which had originally been constructed in 1840 was rebuilt in the same year.

148   *Jeremiah Colman.*

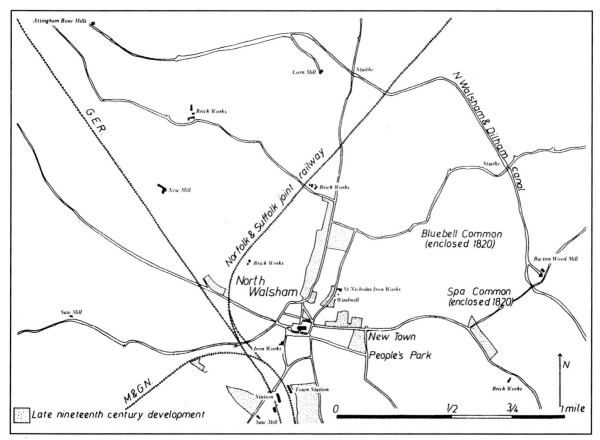

Most of Norfolk's railways still led towards London, and were controlled by the Liverpool Street-based Great Eastern Railway. From the 1870s smaller companies began to develop routes to the Midlands and the north, and in 1893 they were amalgamated into the Midlands and Great Northern Joint Company. Their Norwich station was the now demolished City Station, but their workshops and an important junction point were at Melton Constable built on land owned by Lord Hastings. This settlement is unique in Norfolk as it was entirely created by the railways. Rows of terraced houses were laid out on a gridiron pattern, constructed with building materials brought in by the railway, and the grey Midland brick houses look very alien. Trains left Norwich for Birmingham via Fakenham and King's Lynn and the M. & G.N. developed its own seaside rival to Cromer at Sheringham. The population increased in size from just over a thousand in 1881 to 3,500 in 1911.

149 *19th-century North Walsham.*

A third coastal resort developed by the railways was Mundesley, reached via a line from North Walsham. Although much smaller than its two rivals, it had its share of large hotels and its population doubled between 1881 and 1911. The Norfolk Broads did not become popular as a tourist area until this century, although wildfowlers, yachtsmen and photographers had discovered it by 1900.

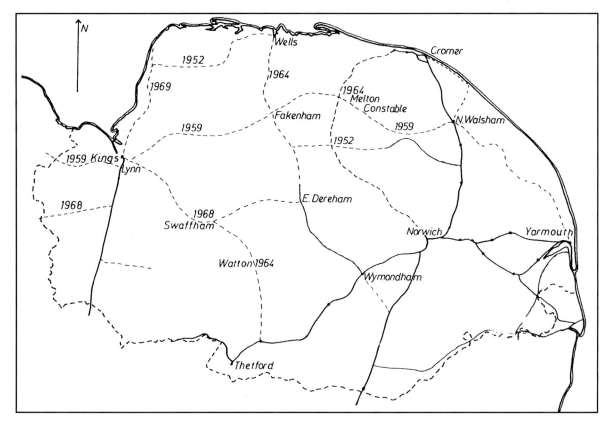

150 *The decline of the railway network.*

North Walsham, which had two stations, one connecting it with Norwich and London, and the other with Lynn and the Midlands, naturally expanded in consequence. The population had reached 4,500 by 1911. There were two iron works, Randells and Cubitts, providing farm machinery, iron and brass castings. A firm of ecclesiastical builders employed craftsmen in stone and wood. New houses were built around the station and to the north towards Swafield, neat Victorian villas and terraces which show how the railways could breathe new life into an old market town.

By the end of the century, Norfolk had changed greatly since the beginning of the Georgian era. From being an industrial and highly populated area with products being made in a large number of prosperous towns and villages, it had become an agricultural county with a stagnating rural population and industry concentrated in Norwich, Yarmouth and a few market towns. It was no longer famous for its wool, but for its tourist attractions. The railways had however brought new life to a number of the towns, which had shown themselves willing and able to adapt to new conditions.

11

Norfolk between the Wars

The 1914-18 war brought irreversible changes to life in Norfolk as else-where. It took a large proportion of the county's young men overseas, and many did not return, as the long lists on local war memorials show. In spite of the squalor and horror of the trenches, some of those taken from the poverty and limited horizons of agricultural labour looked back at the war years as the best of their lives. A South Norfolk man, James Seeley, told the writer George Ewart Evans:

> I think the happiest times I ever had were in the army; though there were real bad times ... when we'd be overtopped with mud and water in the trench, there'd allus be someone say something to make you laugh.

Those who survived came back more aware of the possibility of a better standard of living, and less prepared to put up with old conditions.

Agriculture

The war also had a stimulating effect on agriculture, which had been depressed for nearly forty years. Overseas supplies were disrupted by German submarines, and the government took some control over agriculture. The Corn Production Act was passed and County Agricultural Wages Boards set up. These boards compelled farmers to pay a minimum wage of 25s. a week and the voice of the National Agricultural Labourers and Rural Workers' Union, under the presidency of George Edwards, was heard at county negotiation level.

Even before the war, efforts had begun to improve the depressed state of Norfolk agriculture. The Norfolk Agricultural Station had been founded in 1908 for research and development, and in 1912 sugar beet, which was to revolutionise the farming pattern, was grown experimentally for the first time. Some more unusual new crops were also tried. In 1913 the British Tobacco Growers' Association was set up and crops experi-

151 *Horse ploughing*

mentally grown at Methwold and Croxton. 'If the government had been a little more generous in the matter of granting a small rebate on excise duty for home-grown tobacco, and the big tobacco companies ... more helpful by purchasing the home product, the land utilisation of Breckland might have been different today and many acres which are now forest or heath might have been kept in arable cultivation'. Instead the Forestry Commission was to develop the largest low-land forest in Britain on the light Breckland soils.

In the fenland basic maintenance work continued, but much more effort was needed to improve the drainage system and keep it in good order. By 1913 it was obvious that the sluice at Denver was inadequate, and some districts were frequently flooded and waterlogged. Although various improvement schemes were put forward, none were implemented until after the Second World War. The only modernisation of note was the gradual replacement of steam pumps by oil engines for the work of pumping water into the main drains. Oil engines could be started up quickly and at short notice, and worked faster than steam pumps.

In the years immediately following the First World War an enormous change took place in the system of landholding in the United Kingdom, partly because the agricultural depression made it unprofitable and partly because the death duties introduced by Lloyd George's government reduced the attraction of property-owning as a long-term investment. Between 1918 and 1922 a quarter of England changed hands. Many farms were sold to their tenants who became owner-occupiers. Working farmers had formed only 10 per cent of the owners of farmland in 1914, while by 1927 it had risen to 36 per cent.

Dislocation of international trade continued for some while after the war, and thus foreign competition was slight. By 1921, however, prices began to fall steeply; British farmers were now competing with Canadian wheat, Argentinian beef and New Zealand lamb. The price of wheat dropped from just over 86 shillings a quarter in 1920 to nearly 41 shillings a quarter in 1922. After remaining steady for a few years it then dropped sharply again until conditions began to improve after 1934. The result was a decline in the Norfolk arable crop acreage.

By 1922 wages had fallen back to 22s. a week, and this resulted the next year in one of the few strikes by Norfolk agricultural labourers. The strike ended in a compromise, with wages held at the wartime level of 25s.

The government had at first tried to return agriculture to the free market, but now reversed its policy to one of support. In 1929 agricultural land and buildings were de-rated and wheat growing encouraged by a
152 Single furrow plough made by Randell's of North Walsham
subsidy introduced in 1932. The acreage of wheat in Norfolk increased while that of barley declined until in 1937 the subsidy was extended to cover it. The acreage of other cereal crops declined, particularly rye, the most usual Breckland crop.

Regional variations persisted, in particular those of the Broads, the fens and the Breckland. The Broads remained essentially a summer grazing area and the fens were growing cereals as well as an increasing amount of fruit and vegetables. The intensity of this type of farming

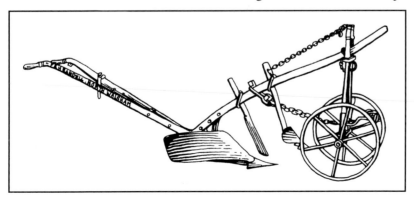

is shown by the fact that in 1921 more farm labourers were employed per 10,000 acres in Marshland Rural District than anywhere else in the county. The next largest employing area was the Flegg area, where holdings were small and cash crops like soft fruit, green vegetables and sugar beet, as well as cereals, were important. In south Norfolk, more land had been put down to grass, partly because of the cost of drainage in a period of depression.

However, during these years when traditional farming patterns were less profitable, there were enterprising producers looking for new crops. By the 1930s, peas, previously grown as fodder and to put nitrogen into the soil, could be sold to canning factories in Wisbech. Orchards and market gardens generally were becoming more important, in the Fleggs, the fens and the Fakenham area. The acreage of potatoes increased by 2,000 to 22,000 between 1926 and 1936, grown mainly in the last-mentioned areas and near Norwich. By 1936 the production of brussels sprouts, cauliflowers, cabbages and carrots had increased substantially.

153 *Turnip cutter made by F. Randell Ltd., North Walsham*

The first modern-style sugar beet factory in England was built at Cantley, near Norwich, in 1921, with a capacity for processing 800 tons a day. A much larger one was built at King's Lynn in 1927, which could process 1,200 tons a day. In 1935 the British Sugar Corporation was established. At certain times the crop could be very labour-intensive. Harvesting involved ploughing out, and then hand pulling, cleaning and topping. These processes were not mechanised until the 1950s. The advantage of sugar beet for the farmer was that it was grown as a cash crop, and acreage increased from 15,015 in 1925 to 95,685 by 1945. It replaced turnips in the crop rotation. The increase in sugar beet growing was matched by a sharp decline in sheep-keeping, which was suffering badly from New Zealand competition.

The decline of horses on farms, which had begun after the introduction of tractors in the early 20th century, continued. Just over 33,000 remained in 1942, but only 14,500 by 1952. Many farmers kept one or two even after they had tractors, for awkward corners, heavy land and for use in wet weather.

The changes in agriculture meant a smaller labour force was required and the number of agricultural workers declined by 10,000 between 1929 and 1942. The decline in the number of horses meant that local harness makers and blacksmiths were no longer required. Bus services to towns meant the end of local tailors and cobblers. The increasing importance of imported wheat led to the closure of village flour mills. A wide range of fertilisers could be bought, and local lime kilns closed; the declining population meant the rural building industry contracted and local brick kilns were redundant. Agriculture was often the only remaining employer, despite its smaller demands, and over much of Norfolk over 50 per cent of the labour force was now permanently employed in agriculture. However, because wages and housing conditions were usually better in towns, now more accessible by bus, bicycle or motor car, many labourers left the land. Others adopted an itinerant work pattern. Some interspersed agricultural work with periods at fertiliser factories like Fisons at Thetford, whilst others went further afield to the breweries of Burton-on-Trent.

Farming conditions remained poor in the 1930s and many farmers went bankrupt, with farms changing hands at very low prices. Henry Williamson purchased his farm on the north Norfolk coast for about £10 an acre in 1936, and a few years later Alan Bloom paid £8 an acre for land in the Fens. Both these very different properties were overgrown and derelict like many others in the county. Rents were also low, less than half the level of the early 1870s when about £1 an acre had been usual. Work on maintaining buildings and hedges, and the weeding of crops were neglected to reduce overheads, which meant that even working farms looked rundown and impoverished. Much poor land reverted to sporting use only, continuing a trend begun in the 19th century.

154 Norfolk horse brasses

Many farmers continued to use traditional methods. The lack of profit was a disincentive to experiment, and many remained suspicious of modern innovations. Dr. Brereton wrote in 1936:

> It is indeed doubtful whether mechanisation is profitable in Norfolk. Where it had been tried it has generally been a failure. In one village in Norfolk three or four men with tractors and drivers displaced 40 labourers. We in Norfolk hold that national wealth is not the only aim of national economy, but also national welfare.

Most farmers since Dr. Brereton have not taken such an altruistic view of the farming industry. Not many farmers had the optimism or the capital of James Keith, who expanded his enterprises throughout the 1930s, so that by 1940 he was farming 17,000 acres. He was prepared to take on land that others did not want, and was largely responsible for land clearance in north-west Norfolk. Between 1938 and 1942, 1,600 acres on Harpley Common, Massingham Heath and Massingham Common were cleared of gorse, bracken and rabbits and by deep ploughing, manuring and heavy liming made to produce good cereal crops. Keith pioneered the growing of lucerne in the Castle Acre area and set up a lucerne meal factory at South Acre. 'Farmer's Glory' breakfast cereal was first manufactured here, to try to provide an outlet for locally grown wheat.

Before the 1914-18 war, Norfolk farmers had taken little serious interest in milk production, but the arrival of Scottish dairy farmers and their Ayrshire cows to take over Norfolk properties generated a new awareness, and by the late 1930s Norfolk was an important milk-producing county. Cattle were, in fact, the only livestock which remained in Norfolk in any numbers. They were grazed on the marshes of the Broads, but many of these were brought in as young stock, particularly from Ireland. About 75 per cent of Broadland was used as grazing in the 1930s and the drainage of the area was constantly improved. Cattle

were looked after by marshmen, who also made sure that the marshes were drained and ditches clean. They also kept a few cows of their own and made and sold butter and cheese. This very lonely life was becoming unpopular by the late 1930s, when there were only about twenty marshmen left, each perhaps looking after 1,000 acres.

In 1931, King George V reintroduced the growing of flax into the county, when three acres were sown near West Newton on the Sandringham estate. By 1933 there were 160 acres and in 1934 a small processing mill was erected, employing 25 men. The Linen Industrial Research Association established a Flax Research Institute nearby at Flitcham Abbey, and between 1935-7 acreage increased by 250 acres. With the outbreak of war it became a government Flax Establishment and output increased dramatically. It reached its peak in 1944 when over 5,000 acres were in production, mostly to be woven into webbing. However, after the war it could not compete with cheaper foreign products and the mill was closed in 1954.

The cultivation of soft fruit had begun as early as the 1890s in the Broads and the fens, but there was a great increase by 1935, encouraged by the establishment of the Norfolk County Council Horticultural Station at Burlingham in 1920, where demonstrations of fruit-growing techniques were given.

Towns, trade and industry

The population of Diss, Fakenham, Swaffham and Thetford declined up to 1931, while elsewhere the population was fairly static. The agricultural depression meant that farmers did not buy or sell so much grain or livestock; it also meant that they had no extra money for the consumer products which the small towns had supplied. This decline of retail trade was accelerated by improved road transport which brought the countryside into easier contact with larger centres. Changes in Aylsham between 1890 and 1933 were typical. The tanner, the agricultural implement maker, the artificial manure manufacturer, the miller, and the cattle cake and seed merchant had all disappeared by 1930. Some retailers, such as the umbrella maker, the tailor and shoemaker had also gone; new enterprises included a motor engineer and a cycle agent. The lack of demand for iron goods, and particularly for agricultural machinery, meant that after the war engineering works which had been engaged in armament production found it difficult to establish a peace-time role. Most of the fifty or so iron foundries in small towns and some villages disappeared, as factory-made goods with standardised parts became more usual.

Changes that helped small-town industry were the introduction of electricity and improved road transport. The existence of a pool of cheap non-union labour in the form of redundant farm workers also encouraged some industries to move in. Printing began in Fakenham in the 1930s; engineering and cabinet making in Dereham; coffee grinding in Thetford; engineering in Cromer and Diss; brushmaking in Wymondham; and canneries and laundry services for coastal hotels in North Walsham.

Thus the role of market towns was changing. Their importance as suppliers of goods and services to their immediate neighbourhood was in decline, but industries geared to national or even international trade increased.

Dereham was the largest market town with a population static at about 5,500 in the early 20th century. It was a railway junction and had a busy market. Previously its industries had been based on agriculture, and included two large maltings and a modern roller flour mill, rebuilt in 1914. Two examples show the way that local industry was changing. Crane's of Dereham began as a wheelwrights and waggon building concern which developed into an agricultural engineering firm. During the First World War it made gun wheels, which led to the growth of a trailer industry after the war. By 1950, 67 per cent of Crane's trailers were exported. Again, in 1932 a Dutch firm manufacturing the cutters needed in the extracting process of the sugar beet industry arrived in Dereham, where it remained until the 1970s.

Other small towns were less fortunate. The closure of Burrells' traction engine works at Thetford was a great loss and Fisons ceased production of super phosphates near the town in 1934. Smaller centres like Swaffham could not attract new industries, and thus depended entirely upon agriculture. When it was in decline they suffered. However, weekly markets were still busy, and so were more specialised ones like the yearly

156 *Norwich shoe industry: outwork between the wars.*

157 *Norwich shoe industry: the machine room at Norvic Shoe Co. Ltd. in the early 1920s.*

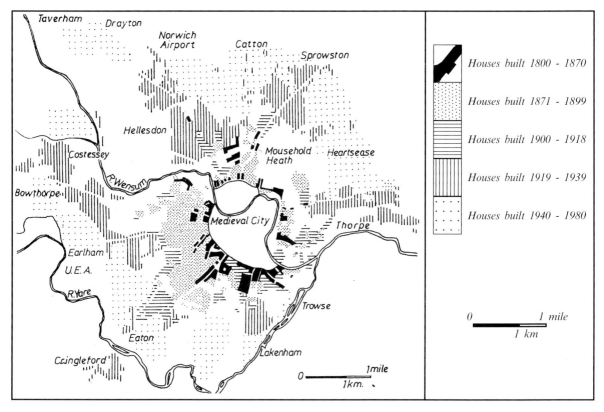

Houses built 1800 - 1870

Houses built 1871 - 1899

Houses built 1900 - 1918

Houses built 1919 - 1939

Houses built 1940 - 1980

158   *The growth of Norwich.*

159   *The Royal Arcade, Norwich,* c.*1900*

Michaelmas turkey sales at Attleborough, where 9,000 live birds were sold in 1934, making it the largest of its kind in the country.

Norwich was still by far the largest, with a population of just over 120,000 throughout the period, and many industries continued to grow. The largest employer was now the boot and shoe industry, with 7,000 employees in 1901. Production methods varied from fully mechanised factories with good working conditions down to the forty or so garret masters still surviving in 1910, who paid very low wages on a casual basis. The last of this group closed in the 1970s.

Food and drink production provided the second largest source of employment, with the Carrow Works alone employing 2,600 people in 1910. Women and young people supplied 65 per cent of the labour. As well as being unskilled, much of this employment was casual. This was true of breweries, jam making and mineral water manufacturing.

There were still two silk mills. Wages were extremely low, with young girls winding and cleaning threads for about three shillings a week. Hindes and Sons remained in business and expanded during the Second World War, producing silk for parachutes. The clothing industry was also a large employer, with a workforce mainly of women and young people. Horse-hair weaving gave about 400 people jobs, often working on hand looms.

Norwich's strength lay both in the variety of her industries and the willingness of these concerns to adapt and diversify, as in the case of the engineering and iron founding firm of Boulton and Paul. It had been manufacturing wire netting since the 1850s, and from 1906 produced engines for small marine craft and a hydroplane was developed. This led the firm into the production of aeroplanes during the First World War and after, although never on a large enough scale to be really profitable. The prefabricated building branch of the firm's activities was more successful, changing its output from elaborate conservatories and bungalows for export to the Empire, to smaller buildings and sheds. Because of its adaptability, the firm survived the 1930s and took on a great deal of heavy engineering work during the Second World War.

Banking and insurance companies—particularly the Norwich Union— survived the years of depression and expanded as conditions began to improve in the late 1930s. Unemployment in Norwich, as elsewhere, was high, reaching a peak of 7,000 men out of a total population of 128,000 in February 1933. However, this figure had halved by summer 1939.

The development of new types of diesel coastal and short-sea vessels led to a revival of Norwich as a port. Cargoes of grain came again; 100,000 quarters a year were being unloaded at Norwich quays by the mid-1930s. Coal and timber were also important cargoes, especially after the riverside electricity power station was opened in 1926.

Housing in Norwich was mostly better than elsewhere and certainly not as overcrowded. Many had gardens. The worst conditions were in the old city. After 1918, local authorities became housing authorities for the first time, and between 1918 and 1923 the first council house estate

160 *Universal Plough-ing Engine from Burrel & Sons, Thetford, 1897.*

in Norwich was built at Mile Cross. From 1924 central government funds were available for housing and this was followed by a period of considerable slum clearance within the city walls and the building of new estates, mostly on the outskirts towards Lakenham in the south, Earlham and Costessey in the west, Hellesdon and Catton to the north and Thorpe to the east. At the same time much of the outer ring road was created. A major project of the years immediately before the Second World War was the building of a new City Hall, which completely changed the appearance of the west end of the Market Place.

The inter-war years were a period of stagnation in Yarmouth where the herring industry was suffering from the overfishing of the North Sea and many of the traditional East European markets were now unavailable. Virtually no home-based ships used the quays in the 1930s. Shipbuilding, once an important industry, had finished by 1933. The only noticeable increase was in coal, on its way to the power station at Norwich after 1926. The growth in the holiday industry did not make up for this loss of port activity and the population declined up to 1951.

King's Lynn fared rather better, trade being helped by improved road communications which increased its importance as a focus of both road and rail networks. Lynn was still the most convenient port between the industrial Midlands and northern Europe. In 1925 a new Anglo-American Oil Depot was built, and between 1926-8 the Alexandra Dock was reconstructed so that it was better suited for modern shipping. The construction of local sugar beet factories meant that the handling of both beet pulp and molasses increased, and by the 1930s new sheds and warehouses had been built.

Expansion of the port, however, was not matched by expansion of the town. The population remained at about 20,000 throughout the period. A major employer was Savage's who had made steam roundabouts and engines since the 1850s. With the declining orders from showmen, however, the firm stagnated in the early 20th century until the Second World War. Other industries were agriculture-related and so suffered from the depression. In spite of its ideal position for exporting goods, Lynn failed to attract new industry, perhaps because its rail connections, though extensive, were slow and circuitous.

By the outbreak of the Second World War, both agriculture and industry were beginning to recover from the worst effects of the depression, and changes which pointed the way to post-war growth were already becoming apparent. The war years interrupted and then accelerated changes which had already begun.

161 *Spad VII fighter plane, made by Mann Egerton & Co. Ltd., Norwich, 1916*

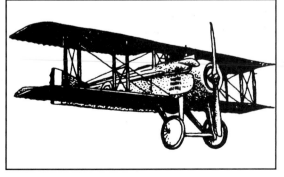

12

The Second World War and After

The outbreak of war brought many changes. Norfolk's position facing Germany meant that it was in the front line for air attack. In July 1940 the bombing of Norwich began, continuing until 1943. In all there were 44 air raids, damaging railway stations and industrial targets as well as much of the central area. The cathedral narrowly escaped, but 11 other places of worship were badly damaged, 340 people were killed and over a thousand injured. Two thousand houses were destroyed and 2,000 more seriously damaged. The only other Norfolk town to suffer seriously from enemy attack was Yarmouth, where much of the medieval town, including the very fine church of St Nicholas, was devastated. There were also frequent attacks on Norfolk air bases, and many spectacular air battles were fought over the county.

There were 63 airfields by 1944, and an influx of soldiers and airmen to man them, matched by a flow of civilians away from the coasts. In June 1940 a coastal belt 20 miles wide was declared a defence area from which visitors were banned. Sea defences were erected and the beaches mined. From July there was a nightly curfew in many areas. Many children and families from London moved into Norfolk villages. Some liked it and stayed after the war; others had returned home within a year. As the war continued and more men were called up, girls came to take their place in the form of the Women's Land Army. As with the evacuees, some settled down in the country rather than return home after the war.

The local economy boomed, with engineering contracts for firms like Boulton and Paul in Norwich, Savage's in King's Lynn and Crane's in Dereham, while textile firms made army uniforms and silk weavers made parachutes. As home food supplies became more important, farming prospered and a massive ploughing campaign began. The speed of mechanisation increased to swell production and compensate for the shortage of labour. Tractors finally replaced horses and in 1931 the first combine harvester arrived at Bluestone farm, South Creake. By 1943 the acreage of wheat had reached a record 142,525 acres, a total not surpassed until the 1960s. Another important development was the introduction of artificial insemination for cattle. The first A.I. station for the region was opened at Beccles in 1943.

162 *Evacuees   at Wymondham station, 1940.*

Each county had a War Agricultural Committee with representatives of farmworkers, landlords and farmers. In February 1940, Norfolk led the way in enforcing a minimum agricultural weekly wage of 38s. A Chief Agricultural Officer, who was normally an agricultural scientist, was appointed in each county, and so greater contact developed between scientists and the farming community. From these beginnings grew today's National Agricultural Advisory Service (A.D.A.S.).

From the late 1950s Norfolk began to gain more population than it lost, and this trend has continued so that between 1971-81 the population grew faster than in any other area of the United Kingdom. Rural population decline, which had typified the countryside in the first half of the century, continued in the 1950s, but by the 1960s population growth gradually spread outwards from the major centres to include large parts of the countryside, even though agriculture and rural industry was in decline. Lower land prices often meant that houses could be erected more cheaply in the countryside, and in the days of cheap oil, commuting might seem financially attractive. People retiring from other areas of Britain could buy a house in a Norfolk village and still have money left over. Advertisements which appeared for bungalows and chalets in Mattishall claimed they were the cheapest in Britain.

Half the settlements in the county still have fewer than 500 inhabitants, and in 170 of these the numbers were still falling up to 1981. Newcomers are not necessarily a bad thing for the community; the problem is, that with large-scale development they all come at once in great numbers and may swamp the existing village rather than become assimilated into it. Retired people often have a lot to contribute; many Women's Institutes, evening classes and church flower-arranging rotas rely on the enthusiasm of these new arrivals. Professional families can be more articulate and less prepared to put up with second-rate services than the locals: the improvement of some village schools, for instance, has been due to pressure from this more vocal type of rural parent. It is inevitable, however, that the newcomers have different expectations of village life than the locals. The older members of the village remember it as an occupational community with common aims and interests, and look back nostalgically; but the demise of these communities cannot be blamed on the new inhabitants.

Villages without newcomers, in fact, are in danger of stagnating or dying altogether. A quarter of Norfolk villages now have no shop and a half no school, both essential for healthy village life. Hundreds of nonconformist chapels are derelict, disused or converted to other uses; and a third of the churches existing in the Middle Ages have disappeared, become ruinous or are redundant. The growing trend towards group practices reduced the number of surgeries by 42 between 1950-80. Most villages no longer have a resident district nurse or policeman. In the first half of the 20th century few places were more than five miles from a railway station; by 1970 the network had been reduced to a few main lines with not even a link between King's Lynn and Norwich. The steady reduction of bus services has left many communities, and especially the non-drivers within them, very isolated indeed. Experiments with community buses have been made, but these have to be subsidised, and run by volunteers; three operate in Norfolk, connecting villages with a local centre three days a week. They are hardly a substitute for proper public transport.

It is county policy to concentrate growth in certain key villages: while economic factors may point to the advantages of channelling population to the 11 per cent of villages with a population of over 1,000, the social benefits of a small community are lost. Socially, it is better to integrate limited numbers of newcomers into small villages rather than create ghettos of outsiders in selected 'growth villages', while the landscape tolerates a few new houses better than large-scale housing estates.

Those who buy weekend cottages pose a worse problem for village society than the newcomers who move in permanently. There is hardly a house on the main street at Cley which is lived in by locals and this is true of many coastal settlements; Burnham Overy is known as 'Cambridge-next-the-sea'. It is true that without weekenders and the tourist industry these villages would be deserted, since the fishing industry has virtually vanished. However, a community must suffer when half its

163 *The changing harvest scene: different methods of straw collecting in the 20th century*

164 *Farm worker, c.1920*

houses are empty during the winter; and the interests of an intermittent holidaymaker will differ from those of a resident local.

Many villages and small towns are recognised as conservation areas, where further developments have to be carefully considered. Although this policy has come too late to save the character of villages like Mattishall, or to prevent the demolition of important buildings like the Norman house in Queen's Street, King's Lynn, there seems hope that these disasters of the past will not be repeated. Recent council housing schemes have shown that high density, relatively cheap development can also be attractive and in keeping with its surroundings. The most ambitious example is the large Bowthorpe development north of Norwich, where a mixture of private and council housing linked to amenities and an industrial site has been built.

In 1950 half of Norfolk's small towns had an agricultural market which brought farmers and their business. Now, however, most have closed and buying and selling is restricted to Norwich. Dereham is an example of an expanding small town, but here little improvement has been made in the centre. The huge new estates at Toftwood built in the 1960s and 1970s mainly house the retired, or Norwich commuters. Most other small towns on main roads have suffered from the building of similar characterless estates, but some more out-of the-way centres like Hingham and Holt retain much of their Georgian and Victorian atmosphere intact. The construction of by-passes, particularly along the busy A11 and A47, greatly improved the urban environment of many small towns in the 1970s. Although there are those who argue that by-passes take away trade, they certainly make places like Dereham, Wymondham and Swaffham far more pleasant.

Until the 1970s the fourteen or so market towns of Norfolk were relatively successful in attracting industry. Towns like Dereham, Fakenham, Swaffham and North Walsham have their own industrial estates. Dereham was unusual in that few new industries came, but pre-war industries like Crane's expanded. In contrast, Diss, on the main railway line to London, attracted a number of new industries and jobs available there doubled between 1961-71. More recently, however, it has been far more difficult to encourage industry to set up in the small towns; many firms have closed down or left the area. In 1971 there were 3,000 fewer non-agricultural jobs for men outside the main towns than in 1961. This figure has increased dramatically since then; between 1976 and 1982 the county has lost 9,000 non-agricultural jobs, mostly in manufacturing.

The fate of the small towns and even more that of the villages is bound up inevitably with the fortunes of agriculture. It is still Norfolk's major industry, but changes over the past 30 years have been faster and greater than ever before. Norfolk is England's most important producer of wheat, barley, sugar beet and many vegetables, and productivity has increased more than in any other industry, through the use of increased mechanisation, fertilisers, herbicides and pesticides, and the production of new strains of seeds. Very often it is only the larger farms which can afford the increased outlay. Nationally the number of smaller farms under 100 acres halved between 1964 and 1982 to 120,000 and it continues to drop. Changes made by the 1976 tenancy laws mean that when a farm becomes vacant the landowner is more likely to amalgamate the farm with other land than to relet it. The Norwich Union Insurance Company began buying land 100 years ago, and now insurance companies and pension funds are the most important landlords in Norfolk. They always aim for the maximum immediate profit, while some local land-owners tend to have more interest in aesthetic improvement, especially if this helps conserve game.

The profitability of wheat was dramatically increased by membership of the E.E.C.; the price went up from £30 a ton to over £100, so it is not surprising that wheat acreages increased by 60 per cent between 1972 and 1982, mainly at the expense of grass. The acreage of barley, a crop for which much of Norfolk is more suited, went down by 12 per cent, although it still grows more than any other county. The acreage of sugar beet has gone up by 25 per cent from 1972-82. Eighty per cent of the total farmland is arable, eight per cent being top-quality and two-thirds being moderate to good. It is only the subsidies available which make continuous cereal production on any but the best soils at all profitable.

The level of financial support for arable farming has undermined the profitability of the livestock sector. Dairy cows and milk production had been increasing from 1939, but after 1951 the number of producers, if not the number of cows, began to fall. The number of herds dropped by half from 1951-61, and after 1972 the number of cows also began to drop and was down to half by 1982. In 1950 a dairy farmer could make a living from 15 cows; to earn the same real income he now needs 75, and the average Norfolk herd is now over a hundred.

The number of sheep kept did not rise significantly until the 1970s. A nine per cent rise in the number of breeding ewes kept may seem surprising during a decade when cereal production was becoming so important, but systems of management which involve feeding sheep on waste from other crops and the use of electric fencing to fold them on the fields, allow them to be kept economically, especially on light soils. E.E.C. and now G.U. subsidies have also provided a stimulus to production.

165 Below left. *Sheep shearing at Holkham as shown on the bas relief on the monument in Holkham Park to Thomas William Coke.*

166 Below. *Inscription above the door at Rollesby House of Industry.*

For the INSTRUCTION of YOUTH
The ENCOURAGEMENT of INDUSTRY
The RELIEF of WANT
The SUPPORT of OLD AGE
And the COMFORT of
INFIRMITY and PAIN.

167 Right. *Hermaph-rodite farm waggon. This cart, convertible into a waggon is unique to Norfolk.*

168 Far right. *Early tractor ploughing*

In spite of market fluctuations, pig numbers have increased steadily since the war, and Norfolk now has the third largest pig herd in England. Only large-scale production is profitable, and 60 per cent of sows are kept in herds of over a hundred. Large mechanised units are typical, although some herds are kept in the open on the light lands.

The most dramatic livestock increase has been in poultry production, where methods have changed completely over the last 30 years. Most laying hens are kept in highly controlled 'battery sheds'; two-thirds are in flocks of over a hundred thousand. Turkey production is similar, and Bernard Matthews is the largest turkey-producer in Europe. Ducklings are a Norfolk speciality, some being kept free-range in the Breckland.

The post-war years have seen a decline in the number of farmworkers employed, due to the increased use of machinery. Few flowers and vegetables still need a large quantity of labour, provided by gangs of women; the Yellow Pages of the telephone directory still list 'gang masters'. The number of people in a bulb field at harvesting time gives some idea of what crowded and busy places fields were before machinery took over.

The use of eight-furrow ploughs, 60-foot wide sprayers, and similar large pieces of equipment has led to efforts to rationalise the field pattern by removing hedgerows. Most of this destruction has been on the heavier lands, where small fields suited to a more pastoral system had survived. This represents not only the loss of ancient boundaries, but also the loss of valuable wild life habitats. The need to maximise output to make the very expensive methods of modern agriculture profitable inevitably leads to conflicts between farmers and environmentalists.

With the increase in cereal production and the new intensive indoor methods of keeping animals, new types of farm building were needed. Grain silos first appeared in the 1950s, and since then huge prefabricated asbestos and concrete barns, animal sheds and poultry housing have come to dominate the Norfolk countryside, most of which do not require planning permission. These factory-style buildings standing amidst wide-open empty fields create a 'prairie' landscape very different from that of even 30 years ago.

The most serious conservation problems have occurred where efforts are made to convert land not normally suitable for cereal production into arable land, a process inevitably involving drastic changes to the environment and ecology. The area over which there has been most controversy was the Broads, where to many the traditional use of marshland for summer grazing still seems the best use to which it can be put. However, ploughing grants and high wheat prices have made it worthwhile to plough and drain this area, releasing chemicals from the lower levels of the peat, which, combining with fertiliser and herbicides, destroy the plant and animal life of the region. The problems in the Broads led to the creation of the first 'Environmentally Sensitive Area'. Now the ESA scheme has been expanded to cover other regions in the U.K.

The fertility and high cropping capacity of the fens are unsurpassed in the United Kingdom, but the problems of keeping them free from water have increased since the war. In March 1947 the melting of the snow after a severe winter combined with heavy rain to inundate 31,000 acres of the South Level. The danger of this becoming a recurring problem led to the digging of a relief channel from Denver to just south of Lynn in the 1950s, and in 1964 a cut-off channel was opened which runs down the east side of the Fens from Mildenhall to Denver (a scheme first proposed by Vermuyden in 1642). Flooding will always be a problem, but that of shrinking and disappearing peat is a still greater one. In dry conditions, 'dust storms' or 'blows' gather force across the bare treeless countryside. If the dry soil catches fire, it can spread beneath the surface, and be almost impossible to extinguish. Without the peat, infertile sands and clays are left; it is essential to develop a method of soil conservation.

In spite of the dominance of cereal farming, the variety of agriculture which was first established by the end of the Middle Ages still exists, with market gardening on the fens and Broads, cereals on the lighter loams and pastoral farming in the south. Many Norfolk views, even in the most intensively farmed areas, still include areas of woodland and groups of old farm buildings. Farmers concerned with the problems of reconciling modern agricultural needs with conservation have joined together in the Farming and Wild Life Advisory Group to publicise ways in which farming methods can be adapted to allow woodland, hedgerows and ponds to be kept. The interest of many farmers and landowners in field sports is an incentive to keep copses and cover for pheasants and foxes. Just over two per cent of Norfolk is in nature reserves. A landscape determined solely by what is most profitable under current conditions would look very different from that which exists today, despite the rapid changes that have taken place.

If the countryside has been through a second agricultural revolution since the war, urban life has changed no less, first enjoying a period of increasing prosperity and then more recently, a drastic decline in employment and industry. The major tasks for the City of Norwich in the 1950s were firstly to rebuild and secondly to place its economy on a peacetime footing. Many factories took the opportunity to move out of the centre to new industrial estates on the city's fringe. The availability of labour and factory sites brought new arrivals, one of the most important being May and Baker (Chemicals).

169 *Norwich City Hall, 1932-8*

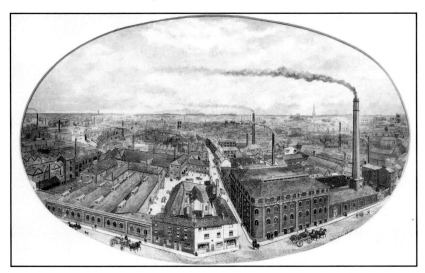

170 Left. *Industrial Norwich with Bullard's brewery in the foreground.*

171 Below. *The Sainsbury Centre, University of East Anglia, opened in 1978.*

The four Norwich breweries had prospered during the war years, but by the end of the 1950s were reduced to two—Bullards, and Steward and Patteson—both of which were taken over by Watney's before 1968. The footwear industry continued to flourish, although many smaller firms went out of business. By 1950 Norwich was the fourth largest producing centre in the United Kingdom, and in 1971 it employed 6,500 people. In the last ten years, however, the industry has been badly hit by cheap foreign imports, and many firms have been forced to close or reduce production. The same is true of engineering firms like Laurence Scott, and Boulton and Paul.

In post-war Norwich only one firm was engaged in the city's traditional industry of textile production. St Mary's silk mills suffered war damage, but were expanded and rebuilt to produce nylon, with a small amount of silk for export. The firm was taken over by Courtaulds in 1964 and continued to expand until 1968. Thereafter it declined; Courtaulds finally closed it in 1980.

Non-productive service industries, such as Norwich's major employer, the Norwich Union, have suffered least from the recession. The government has resited both Her Majesty's Stationery Office and the Civil Service Central Computer Agency in Norwich, although both have had to cut back on jobs in recent years. Superstores have also provided new employment opportunities. East Anglian Independent Television is based in the city and has helped to emphasise the city's regional role, as has the growing importance of Norwich Airport and the establishment of the University of East Anglia, both on the outskirts of the city.

The port declined in the 1960s and its business was further reduced by the closure of the gas works in 1973 when coal ceased to come upriver by boat. Grain boats still use the port, and if, as is hoped, the role of smaller boats increases, it may gain in importance once again. Bridges for the new southern by-pass are planned to allow clearance of medium-sized cargo vessels.

Other large Norfolk towns also shared in the post-war prosperity. In spite of the final collapse of the herring industries, Yarmouth expanded in new directions, including food processing and the development of radio engineering. In the 1960s, however, the port activities were of the greatest importance. Shell-Mex opened an enlarged oil depot in 1947, and expanded it again in 1956, and even more significantly, Yarmouth was selected as a supply base for North Sea Gas. By the early 1970s 2,000 new jobs had been created. As roll-on, roll-off facilities were developed general port activities also increased, but improved road links and more investment are needed for further development. Many of the post-war industries have declined recently; Smiths' Crisps and Birds Eye Walls have both closed their factories. Competition from foreign 'packages' has hit the holiday trade. In 1991, Yarmouth was the area of highest unemployment in Norfolk.

King's Lynn and Thetford have both expanded since the war as the result of schemes supported by the London County Council which began in the early 1960s. After 1962 over fifty new enterprises, many associated with food processing, opened in King's Lynn, and the population rose to just under thirty thousand between 1961-71, a growth accompanied by development of the port. Between 1963 and 1969, the tonnage of cargoes continually increased. There are regular roll-on, roll-off services to much of northern Europe, and more development in this direction is likely, although an improved A47 link to the Midlands is needed.

The development of Thetford resulted in a 15 per cent per annum rise in the amount of employment between 1959-69 and a population increase of 7,500. Expansion has continued since and the population is nearing twenty thousand in 1981. Good road links have helped development.

Tourism has been a growth industry since the war, not only in the old-established centres, but all along the coast and more recently, inland.

172 *North Sea oil rig.*

173 *Pavilion, Great Yarmouth*

At the peak of the season, holidaymakers form a quarter of the county's population. The coast to the north of Yarmouth as far as Hemsby and intermittently thereafter to Mundesley is an example of how damaging badly-sited caravan parks and holiday chalets can be; but fortunately the rest of the coast, except those areas immediately adjoining holiday centres, has suffered less seriously. The Broads is the other area to have suffered severely from the influx of visitors. In 1945 there were 495 boats for hire, very few motorised; today there are well over 2,000 and most are large motor launches. The turbulence they create damages river banks, washing off sediment which silts up the rivers, and destroys animal habitats. About one million visitors come to the Broads every year. It is important that Norfolk's beautiful coastline, historic towns and villages and wide empty landscapes are not spoilt by the very visitors who come to see them.

By 1945 most rural roads were surfaced and between 1966-75 traffic increased by a quarter on trunk roads and nearly a half on principal roads. The cuts in rail services have accelerated this trend. Recent developments have improved the situation, with the provision of by-passes, and the construction of the M11, for instance. Nevertheless, there are plenty of Norfolk people who would argue that road improvements have gone far enough. We do not want to make it too easy for others to enter the county!

The history of Norfolk is a long and varied one, but the greatest changes have taken place over the last 40 years. Although the local economy now seems to be stabilising, there is little prospect of an immediate upturn. More emphasis may have to be laid on the provision of amenities for leisure and holidaymakers, than on the encouragement of new industries. Change is essential and inevitable, although it would be a tragedy for Norfolk to lose its individuality, which it has retained through its isolation from industrial Britain: 'Norfolk is not quite so busy, not quite so overcrowded, and not quite so characterless as some other parts of the country'. With careful planning and a concern for long-term prosperity rather than short-term profit, it should be possible to retain much of value from the past, whilst adapting for the future. The wide views of gently rolling landscapes, nearly always containing a fine medieval church tower and a clump of trees around a 19th-century marl pit, so much admired by Cotman and his fellow artists, still inspire painters today. Well-farmed and cared-for fields indicating the source of the county's wealth over the centuries may look established and eternal, but in fact modern man has the ability to preserve or destroy. It is the maintenance of this fragile balance between conservation and change which is the unenviable responsibility of the present generation. Let us hope for the sake of those who follow us that we get it right!

Bibliography

General Works

Atherton, I., *et al* (eds.), *Norwich Cathedral, Church, City and Diocese 1096-1996* (1996)

Ayres, B., *Norwich* (1994)

Blake, P.W., *et al., The Norfolk we live in (1956)*

Boston, N., and Puddy, E., *Dereham* (1952)

Briers, F., (ed.), *Norwich and its Region* (1961)

Clarke, W.G. (revised by Clarke, R.R.), *In Breckland Wilds* (1937)

Green, B., and Young, R., *Norwich, the Growth of a City* (1981)

Darby, H.C., *The Changing Fenland* (1983)

Darroch, E., and Taylor, B., *A Bibliography of Norfolk History* (1975)

Dymond, D., *The Norfolk Landscape* (1985)

Kenworthy, J., *et al., Burke's and Saville's Guide to Country Houses: vol. III, East Anglia* (1981)

Lawson, A., 'The archaeology of Witton', *East Anglian Archaeology*, vol. 18 (1983)

Margeson, S., Ayres, B., and Heywood, S., *A Festival of Norfolk Archaeology* (1996)

Pevsner, N.B.L., *North-East Norfolk and Norwich* (Buildings of England, 1962)

Pevsner, N.B.L., *North-West and South Norfolk* (Buildings of England, 1962)

Pocock, T., *Norfolk* (1995)

Puddy, E., *Litcham: the Short History of a Mid-Norfolk Village* (1958)

Pursehouse, E., *Waveney Valley Studies* (1966)

Richards, P., *King's Lynn* (1990)

Rose, E., and Robinson, B., *Norfolk Origins 2: Roads and Tracks* (1983)

Taylor, B., *A Bibliography of Norfolk History* II (1991)

Wade Martins, P. (ed.), *Norfolk from the Air*, (1987)

Wade Martins, P. (ed.), *An Historical Atlas of Norfolk* (2nd. ed. 1994)

Wren, W.J., *Ports of the Eastern Counties* (1976)

Yaxley, D., *Portrait of Norfolk* (1977)

Periodicals

East Anglian Archaeology, 1976-
Norfolk Archaeology, 1847-
Norfolk Industrial Archaeology Journal of, 1971-

Prehistoric

Ashbee, P., and Barringer, C.J. (eds.), *Aspects of East Anglican Prehistory* (1984)

Clarke, R.R., *East Anglia* (1960)

Lawson, A., Martin, E., and Priddy, D., 'The barrows of East Anglia', *East Anglian Archaeology*, vol. 12 (1981)

Mercer, R.J., *Grimes Graves, Norfolk: excavations 1971-2* (1981)

Robinson, B., *Norfolk Origins 1: Hunters to First Farmers* (1981)

Roman and Pagan Saxon

Gelling, M., *Signposts to the Past* (1978)

Green, C., *Sutton Hoo; The Excavation of a Royal Ship Burial* (1963)

Hills, C., 'The Anglo-Saxon cemetery at Spong Hill, North Elmham, Part I', *East Anglian Archaeology*, vol. 6 (1977)

Hills, C., and Penn, K., 'The Anglo-Saxon cemetery at Spong Hill, North Elmham, Part II', *East Anglian Archaeology*, vol. 11 (1981)

Hills, C., and Penn, K. and Rickett, R., 'The Anglo-Saxon Cemetery at Spong Hill, North Elmham, Part III', *East Anglian Archaeology*, vol. 21 (1984)

Johnson, S., *The Roman Forts of the Saxon Shore* (1967)

Johnson, S., 'Burgh Castle: Excavations by Charles Green 1958-61', *East Anglian Archaeology*, vol. 20 (1983)

Margary, I.D., *Roman Roads in Britain* (1967)

Myres, J.N.L., and Green, B., *The Anglo-Saxon Cemeteries of Caistor-by-Norwich and Markshall, Norfolk* (1973)

Philips, C.W. (ed.), *Fenland in Roman Times* (1970)

Wacher, J., *The Towns of Roman Britain* (1974)

Webster, G., *Boudicca* (1978)

Williamson, T., *Origins of Norfolk* (1993)

The Coming of Christianity

Carter, A., 'The Anglo-Saxon origins of Norwich: the problems and approaches', *Anglo-Saxon England*, vol. 7 (1978)

Gallyon, M., *The Early Church in Eastern England* (1973)

Taylor, H.M., and Taylor, J., *Anglo-Saxon Architecture*, 3 vols. (1965)

Wade Martins, P., 'Excavations in North Elmham Park', *East Anglian Archaeology*, vol. 9 (1980)

Whitelock, D., 'The pre-Viking Church in East Anglia', in Clemoes, P., *Anglo-Saxon England* (1972)

The Middle Ages

Allison, K.J., 'The lost villages of Norfolk', *Norfolk Archaeology*, vol. 31 (1958)

Ayers, B., and Lawson, A., *Digging under the Doorstep* (1983)

Bennett, M.S., *The Pastons and their England* (1922)

Carter, A. and Clarke, H., *Excavations in King's Lynn, 1963-70* (1977)

Darby, H.C., *The Domesday Geography of Eastern England* (1952)

Darby, H.C., *The Medieval Fenland* (1974)

Davenport, F.G., *The Economic Development of a Norfolk Manor, 1086-1565* (1906)

Doubleday, H.A., and Page, W. (ed.), *Victoria County History of Norfolk*, vol. II (1906)

Dickinson, J.C., *The Shrine of Our Lady of Walsingham* (1956)

Ecclestine, A.W. and J.L., *The Rise of Great Yarmouth* (1959)

Fawcett, R., *The Architecture and Furnishing of Norfolk Churches* (1974)

Gillchrist, R. and Oliva, M., *Religious women in Medieval East Anglia* (1993)

Hedges, A.A.C., *Yarmouth is an Ancient Town* (1959)

Julian of Norwich, *Revelations of Divine Love*, Penguin edition (1966)

Lambert, J.M., *et al.*, *The Making of the Broads* (1960)

Morris, J. (general ed.), *Domesday Book: Norfolk* (1984)

Parker, V., *The Making of King's Lynn* (1971)

Wade Martins, P., 'Fieldwork and Excavations on a Village Site in Launditch Hundred', *East Anglian Archaeology*, vol. 10 (1980)

Yaxley, D., 'Documentary evidence for North Elmham', in Wade Martins, P., 'Excavations in North Elmham Park, II', *East Anglian Archaeology*, vol. 9 (1980)

Tudors and Stuarts

Allison, K.J., 'The sheep-corn husbandry of Norofolk in the 16th and 17th centuries', *Agricultural History Review*, vol. 5 (1957)

Allison, K.J., 'Flock management in the 16th and 17th centuries', *Economic History Review*, 2nd. ser., vol. 11 (1958)

Darby, H.C., *The Draining of the Fens* (1940)

Hassell-Smith, A., *County and Court* (1974)

James, C.W., *Chief Justice Coke, his Family and Descendants at Holkham* (1929)

Ketton-Cremer, R.W., *Norfolk in the Civil War* (1969)

Land S., *Kett's Rebellion* (1977)

Pound, J.P., *The Norwich Census of the Poor*, 1570 (1971)

Simpson, A., *The Wealth of the Gentry, 1540-1660: East Anglian Studies* (1961)

Thirsk, J., 'Norfolk and Suffolk', in Thirsk, J. (ed.), *The Agrarain History of England and Wales: vol. V, part I, 1500-1640* (1967)

Yaxley, D., and Virgoe, N., *The Manor House in Norfolk* (1978)

Yaxley, S., *Tudor Home Life* (1980)

Georgian and Victorian Times

Armstrong, B.J., *Norfolk Diary* (1949 and 1963)

Bacon, R.N., *The Agriculture of Norfolk* (1844)

Barnes, P., *Norfolk Landowners since 1880* (1993)

Chadwick, O., *A Victorian Miniature* (1961)

Crowley, J., and Reid, A. (eds.), *The Poor Law in Norfolk 1700-1850: a Collection of Source Material* (1983)

Digby, A., *Pauper Palaces* (1978)

Ede, J., Virgoe, N., and Williamson, T., *Halls of Zion, Chapels and Meeting Houses in Norfolk* (1994)

Edwards, G., *From Crowscaring to Westminster* (1922)

Goreham, G., *Georgian Norwich* (1972)

Gordon, D.I., *A Regional History of the Railways of Great Britain: vol. 5, The Eastern Counties* (1968)

Groves, R., *Sharpen the sickle! The History of the Farm Workers' Union* (1949)

Haggard, H.R., *A Farmer's Year* (1899)

Haggard, L.R., *I Walked by Night* (1935)

Haggard, L.R., *The Rabbitskin Cap* (1939)

Hemingway, A., *The Norwich School of Painters, 1803-33* (1979)

Hepworth, P., *Victorian and Edwardian Norfolk from Old Photographs* (1972)

Hobsbawm, E.J. and Rudé, G., *Captain Swing* (1969)

Livingstone, S., *A Penny a Boy* (1978)

Mardle, J., *Victorian Norfolk* (1981)

Moore, A., *The Norwich School of Artists* (1995)

Parker, R.C., *Coke of Norfolk and the Agricultural Revolution* (1975)

Peacock, A.J., *Bread or Blood: a study of the Agrarian Riots in East Anglia in 1816* (1965)

Riches, N., (revised ed.), *The Agricultural Revolution in Norfolk* (1967)

Rouse, M., *Coastal resorts of East Anglia* (1982)

Springall, M., *Labouring Life in Norfolk Villages, 1834-1914* (1936)

Stirling, A.M.W., *Coke of Norfolk and his Friends* (2 vols., 1908)

Taigel, A., and Williamson, A.T., *Gardens in Norfolk* (1990)

Wade Martins, S., *A Great Estate at Work* (1980)

Wade Martins, S., *Norfolk, a Changing Countryside* (1988)

Wade Martins, S., *Turnip Townshend* (1990)

White, W., *White's Directory of Norfolk, 1845* (reprinted 1974)

Woodforde, J., *The Diary of a Country Parson, 1758-1802* (1924-31)

Young, A., *A General View of the Agriculture of the County of Norfok* (1804)

The Twentieth Century

Banger, J.R., *Norwich at War* (1974)

Baird, W.W., and Tarrant, J.K., *Hedgerow Destruction in Norfolk, 1946-70* (1973)

Farley, V., *Pictures from a Village* (1981)

Hawkins, C.B., *Norwich: a Social Study* (1910)

Hutchinson, J., and Owers, A.C., *Change and Innovation in Norfolk Farming* (1980)

James, Z. (ed.), *Within Living Memory: a Collection of Norfolk Reminis-cences* (1972)

Norfolk County Council Planning Department, *Norfolk Joint Structure Plan: A Survey* (1974)

Norwich Corporation, *City of Norwich Plan* (1945)

Williamson, H., *The Story of a Norfolk Farm* (1941)

Index